Paralyzed without fear

A Family of Their Own

by Jacqueline Dunkle
with Erik and Jennifer Fugunt

Second Edition

Second Edition © Copyright 2019
Second Edition Cover and Book Design by Jacqueline Dunkle
Second Edition Cover Photo by *Photography With Flair* – Jenn Arnold

First Edition © Copyright 2015
First Edition Cover and Book Design by Donnia Denig
First Edition Cover Photo by *It's A Feeling Photography* – Genie Rogers

Afterword transcribed from interview with Ronda Barrett, Personal Historian
www.honoryourstory.com

Technical Support: Kelly Kahle Simonette

ISBN-13: 9781696256681

DISCLAIMER
This book is designed to provide helpful information and motivation to our readers. This book is not meant to be used, nor should it be used, to diagnose or treat any medical condition. For diagnosis or treatment of any medical problem, consult your own physician. This book is sold with the understanding that the author(s) is not engaged to render any type of medical, legal, or any other kind of professional advice. The content is the sole expression and opinion of its author(s). No warranties or guarantees are expressed or implied. Neither the publisher nor the individual author(s) shall be liable for any damages or negative consequences from any treatment, action, application or preparation, to any person reading or following the information in this book. References are provided for informational purposes only and do not constitute endorsement of any websites or other sources. Readers should be aware that the websites listed in this book may change. Our views and rights are the same: You are responsible for your own choices, actions, and results.

table of contents

foreword by Jennifer Fugunt

01   - purpose

02   - brave enough

03   - pooping

04   - damn garbage

05   - purgatory

06   - swimmers

07   - aghast

08   - a glimpse

09   - shock and awe

10   - gizmo

11   - hand of god

12   - take two

13   - still alive

14   - special powers

15   - glows in the dark

16   - family bonds

17   - surprize

18   - eyes

afterword by Erik Fugunt

with special thanks

Male Fertility Research Program at The Miami Project to
Cure Paralysis www.miamiproject.miami.edu

Erik M. Pelton & Associates, PLLC
www.erikpelton.com

University of Kentucky / Frazier Rehabilitation Institute
Partnership www.victoryoverparalysis.org

Tanya Rivera / WFMY News 2 Anchor

Christopher & Dana Reeve Foundation
www.christopherreeve.org

North Carolina Assistive Technology Program's Grant
Advisory Council for Stephen E. Sallee Award of
Excellence

New Hanover Regional Medical
Center Wilmington, North Carolina

Alamance Regional Medical Center / Cone Health
Burlington, North Carolina

T&T Technology's Standing Wheelchair / Raleigh NC

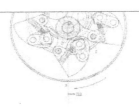

dedication

Jennifer Jugunt

my son's wife
and love of his life

my daughter-in-love

and the perfect mother
for my grandchildren

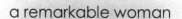

a remarkable woman

foreword
by Jennifer Fugunt

"Timing is everything.
I'm looking at the
clock, calendar
and ovulation test strips
with agonizing fear.
I look again at my
biological clock
like it's on the wall
staring back at me,
a constant reminder
that my time is up
even though I'm only
in my late twenties."

That was a timeline that I'd given myself. All women have a time frame for important events in their lives. Most of the events in my life had gone according to plan but this one was out of my hands. I once read a poem that said family is a place to laugh, grow and yell. Now that seemed like a place that I would never get to visit. Our home was just a house that felt empty without the pitter patter of baby feet.

My mother-in-law Jacque's first book, *Gratitude & Grit - A Mother's Healing Journey* tells the touching story of her son Erik's motorcycle accident, recovery and survival as a paraplegic. That book ends with a goal and hope that Erik and I shared to have a family of our own despite Erik's paralysis. This sequel shares our story through the eyes of my mother-in-law; a listener, motivator and rock on our journey to parenthood.

My husband Erik and I have grown close from being forced to overcome obstacles that many won't experience in a lifetime, in situations where there seemed to be no light at the end of the tunnel. Life presents barriers that can keep you from success. Fear of failure will set in. But when triumph is the only option you choose, you can't lose. With the support from everyone in our family, we turned fear into bravery,

and the outcome became three miracles.

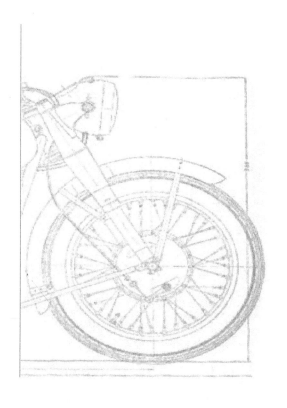

"Everyone is handed adversity in life.

No one's journey is easy.

It's how they handle it that makes people unique."

~ Kevin Conroy

01 | purpose

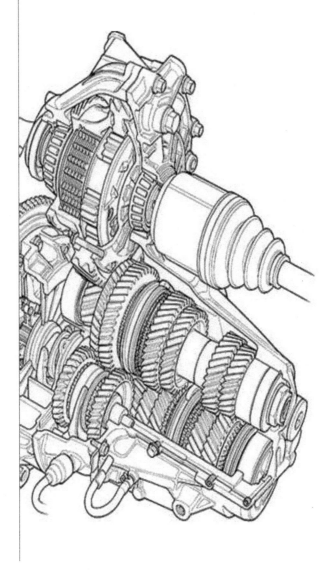

My son, Erik Wolfgang Fugunt was born on the Fourth of July, 1984. It was quite an appropriate day for his birth ~ symbolic of independence and fireworks.

What I remember most about his infancy was that he hated to crawl. He wanted to walk and even appeared enticed by the possible danger of falling. He relentlessly pulled his tiny body up to the coffee table over and over again until he mastered standing. By the age of nine months he had achieved his independence. He could walk. Before long he was doing a whole lot more than walking, henceforth the fireworks began on a daily basis.

Erik was just a year old when his father gave him his first mini bike, a used Honda 50. Ron, a diehard adventurer, cleverly welded an old red Radio Flyer wagon to the side of the mini bike so little Erik could ride it without tipping over. My son was fearless from the get-go and was constantly tearing things apart to find out how they worked; then he'd fabricate gadgets or elaborate mousetrap-like contraptions using the knowledge from his findings.

Like his father, he was a natural gearhead and whether I liked it or not, Erik also became a diehard adventurer. The boys outnumbered me from day one and it didn't take long for me to realize that my life would be anything but boring.

My son also inherited his father's risk-taking personality and my perseverance, a combination of traits that made any attempt to alter his spirit absolutely futile. The only thing that got me through Erik's youth was my faith in God. It was obvious that my son's life began in my womb; but it was always in God's hands.

I soon began to realize that the only impact I would have in Erik's life would be through God's influence. So I quickly taught him the Lord's Prayer and we'd talk about the mystical man in the picture that I kept in his room, the picture Jesus.

When Erik was five years old, his great-grandmother Sara died and I gently explained that she was in Heaven now, with Jesus. About a week later, little Erik came to me with a butter knife in hand and said, ever so casually, "I think I should kill myself now, so I can be in Heaven with Grandma and Jesus." Once again, I explained that it wasn't time for him to go to Heaven and that God would decide that time. I assured him that we wanted him to be here with us for a very long time.

"Dear God," I prayed silently, "My beautiful little boy is not afraid to die. I beg of you, please watch over him. Jesus, please watch over him and guide him. He is your child before he is mine."

Ron and I divorced when Erik was nine years old, not a pleasant time for any of us, especially a little boy caught in the line of fire. Three years later, Erik and his father moved from Pennsylvania to North Carolina. I immersed myself in work to help me ignore the heartache of being so far away from my only child but every now and then I'd catch wind of his most recent antics. Honestly, it's a wonder that I didn't have a stroke. I guess every parent experiences some type of worry regarding their child. My child just seemed to ratchet that worry to the nth degree.

By his 21st birthday, Erik was living in Easton, Maryland where I visited him to celebrate the fact that he survived his youth. As we sat on a park bench together and watched people pass by, he took me by surprise when he nonchalantly said, "I can sense in my gut when people have evil in their hearts. I know when they're up to no good. See that guy over there?" He nodded in the direction of a fellow walking down the street. "He's up to no good. And see that lady there?" He nodded in the other direction. "She's a sweet little old lady that has no idea he's up to no good. It's like I know when I need to watch out for others." We watched the guy that was allegedly up to no good disappear around the corner and then we smiled at the sweet little old lady as she passed in front of us.

"Mom, I feel like I was sent here for a purpose,

like I was born to do something really important
that could change the course of the world
and it feels like it might be tragic.

Do you know what I mean?"

"Yes," I comfortably replied, as if we'd had this conversation in another lifetime. "I know exactly what you mean. I have the same feeling. Sometimes I feel like the mother in that movie, Terminator 2: Judgment Day, trying desperately to keep her son safe so he can fulfill his purpose. I believe you have something very important to do during this lifetime, something that could change the course of the world. I can't explain it. I just feel it. I just know it." We sat in silence for a few moments before Erik spoke again.

"Do you think you know it when it happens,

when you've done that which you're sent here to do?"

I pondered his prophecy for a few moments before I answered, "I don't know, Erik. I don't know if we're supposed to know when it happens."

We got up from the park bench in a state of reverie and moseyed down the sidewalk into a Goodwill store to look for undiscovered treasures. As we played with our potential finds, an old fur coat and a wet suit, I noticed that a very unusual man had stopped his own treasure hunt and had begun to watch our game of hunt. He smiled kindly as he approached us, tilted his head and looked directly into Erik's eyes.

His voice was soft and kind when he finally spoke. "I haven't seen eyes that deep for a long time. Your son has the eyes of Jesus, so humble." Then he looked at me in my Goodwill play clothes and flattered my ego with his observation by adding, "And that fur looks stunning with your hair!" I laughed at his remark about the fur. But I was completely taken back with his comment about Erik's eyes.

I have to admit, I often joked about the way strangers are drawn to Erik and I'd tease that they must feel baby Jesus love coming from his heart. Still, it was just a joke. Yes, Erik's eyes definitely had a language all their own, but the eyes of Jesus? Uh, I don't think so.

After a lengthy conversation with this Goodwill stranger about his ongoing work for God, he gave each of us a Saint Benedict crucifix for protection and wished us Godspeed. We weren't Catholic but we didn't need to be to know that something profoundly unusual had occurred that day. Both Erik and I were so emotionally affected by our encounter with this stranger that we couldn't even speak of it. We just knew it, felt it, saw it in each other's eyes. It was as if we both were awakened to the sobering realization that a special journey had been planned for us; we knew we had to accept the travel arrangements without knowing the destination.

Erik and I had a lot of spiritual conversations after that encounter. One of particular significance took place four years later in May of 2009, when I called him to tell him about a horrible accident that hit close to home. My best friend Lori's son had died when he was thrown from the back of a pickup truck. I sobbed into the phone and confessed, "I always thought it would be me who got the call that my son had been killed in an accident."

"Yeah, me too," Erik replied. "I don't know how I've walked away from all my crashes. I've been banged up a little but always able to walk away. I just want you to know that if you ever do get that call, I'll be okay. I'm not afraid to die. And remember that I love the ocean. That's where you'll feel me most and that's where you'll always be able to find me. Don't worry, Mom. I love you. Everything will be okay." As I cried for my friend Lori and her son, I also cried for myself. I thought maybe I had dodged the bullet and had somehow been spared from receiving that dreaded phone call. Maybe my best friend had taken my place in fate's line of fire.

As Lori's grief raged, I found myself in a strange place that closely resembled guilt, but not for long. It was only eleven months later, on April 14th, 2010, that I received the call I always feared would come. I fell to my knees when I received the news that my son was in ICU and not expected to live. He had crashed his motorcycle on his way home from morning classes at Cape Fear Community College. I hadn't dodged that fated bullet after all. It had been fired twice and this time I took the direct hit.

How could this happen? How could my best friend Lori and I both get the call? What the hell was going on? As I raced six hundred miles from Pennsylvania toward the coast of North Carolina to hold my son before he died, his words replayed over and over in my mind.

"I just want you to know that if you ever do get that call, I'll be okay.

I'm not afraid to die.

And remember that I love the ocean ~

~ that's where you'll
feel me most and that's
where you'll always be able
to find me.

**Don't worry Mom. I love you.
Everything will be okay."**

Somewhere in my unspeakable despair, I had already accepted Erik's imminent death and the closer I got to the ocean, the more I felt his spirit. His own words had prepared me for his death; but neither of us were prepared for the miraculous sequence of events in the Trauma ER, which by the grace of God, resulted in an unexpected outcome.

Erik survived, but his body paid a terrible price. Along with many other life-threatening injuries, a portion of his thoracic spinal column was crushed and a shard of vertebra was literally wedged into his spinal cord. He was completely paralyzed from the chest down. Life the way we knew it ~ life the way he lived it ~ had ended.

That little boy who had spent his life skillfully pushing the boundaries, gracefully balancing on the edge, suddenly became a man who could no longer walk. In fact, from the chest down, his body could no longer do anything it used to do.

So now what? The questions raced through my mind. Would he accept his paralysis or become a statistic of those who can't accept it and choose not to live? And what about his new girlfriend, Jennifer, whom I'd met for the very first time in the ICU waiting room? Would she be able to handle this unexpected twist of fate? Or would she break it off? If she did break it off, would he end his life?

My mind was a whirling tornado of "what ifs" as I whispered a familiar prayer from the eye of the storm. "Dear God, my beautiful little boy is not afraid to die. I beg of you, please watch over him. Jesus, please watch over him and guide him. He is your child before he is mine."

April 2010

Erik and Jennifer on a date
at the Azalea Festival
in Wilmington, NC

a few days before the
motorcycle accident that
rendered him a paraplegic

02 brave enough

I stayed with Erik for six weeks after he was discharged from rehab while he continued to recover at Jennifer's house in North Carolina. I'd been with him virtually every day since his accident for a total of fourteen weeks. He was sick of me in his face and in his space, day in and day out, and scoffed at the notion of maintaining a traditional rehab exercise routine. The dangling carrot that enticed him to regain a sense of self was the ability to drive again. Given his background, that was a no-brainer. He had the need for speed, always.

We arranged for a disabled driver evaluation as soon as possible. The hardest part of the process for Erik was getting into the evaluator's car. He was still healing from all his injuries as well as lugging around a vacuum pump that was connected to an open incision in his back. Once he finally got himself transferred into the car, he passed the driver's test with ease. That was a no-brainer too. He had used hand controls all his life on motorcycles.

We immediately scheduled an appointment for hand controls to be installed in Erik's own car and within three months of his accident, he was on the road again. It was time for me to go. As soon as he was able to drive, I headed for Pennsylvania and home. Weary and worn, I certainly was ready to go, but not ready to let go.

I knew Erik wasn't afraid to die.
He'd proven that many times over.

But was he brave enough to live?

No one plans on becoming paralyzed and spending the rest of their life in a wheelchair. Erik was no different. Paralysis, unlike death, was an unacceptable outcome of risky behavior and a bigger challenge than he had opted for. He had come up with an exit plan and his friend had made a pact to help him execute it.

When Erik reached the decision to act upon the plan, his friend skillfully bargained and struck a better deal. He asked Erik for a grace period and said, "I want you to be sure. If you still feel this way in five years, then I promise, I'll do it."

That friend's negotiated grace period bought us some time; but I was still concerned about Erik's safety. Now that he could drive, he had the means to kill himself easily. He certainly had his life in his own hands and was able to decide life or death for himself. He needed a reason to live and time to find his own way. I sensed that Jennifer would play a critical part in his journey, no matter how their future evolved together.

Erik Fugunt ▶ **Jennifer**

June 24. 2010

The pain of standing beside me while I was struggling for life, knowing the odds were against me and that any moment could have been our last together were no doubt more difficult than anything I could ever imagine. To be completely honest it was the most devoted, kind, brave and selfless act I have ever had the honor to be a part of. Although I could only hear your voice, I want you to know that I fought for us and you are the reason I am here. I was, am, and forever will be yours. I love you and am in your debt for being so incredibly strong in my time of need. I pray every day that somehow, someway I will get a chance to repay the courage, love and undying faith for our relationship that you have shown for it. I love you.

After reading that testimony of love, I knew that when Jenny insisted Erik move directly into her house after eight weeks of rehabilitation, she was undoubtedly the best thing for him. She lived in Mebane, which was a few hours from their home town of Wilmington; so they'd be on their own, away from friends and family, and would have to depend on each other to get through this. I am indebted to Jenny for remaining faithful to Erik during his recovery. Her unwavering commitment was astounding. I just wasn't sure if her pledge could withstand the test of time or if she could maneuver the obstacles of life with a paraplegic. A mother's love is unconditional; she could accept the circumstances without batting an eyelash; but a girlfriend is different. A girlfriend has a choice. Jenny had chosen to accept the circumstances ~ for now. Erik and Jenny's courtship prior to the accident had only been a brief two months, but they had already discussed their mutual and deep desire to have a family together. First and foremost, they both wanted children ~ a family of their own.

Erik's paralysis from the chest down left him unable to conceive a child the old fashioned way, via natural intercourse. And since neither of them would consider adoption, the opportunity for them to become parents was not as promising as they had first thought. The grateful excitement of Erik's survival soon gave way to the grueling reality of paralysis as they began the arduous process of rebuilding their lives, facing the obstacles and unknowns ~ together.

While those of us that loved them stood back and wondered how they could possibly be thinking about babies in the midst of their situation, Erik and Jenny stayed the course in searching for conception help. In August of 2010, four months after Erik's crash, Jenny learned about a research program in Florida that worked specifically with paralyzed people and male fertility issues. She immediately applied to the program which was conducted by The Miami Project to Cure Paralysis. They waited for an invitation for Erik to participate but a response never came. To say they were disappointed would be a gross understatement. They were hoping for help from a facility that would offer goodwill fertility services because of their limited financial resources, but they remained faithful to the pursuit of a family despite the lack of a response from The Miami Project.

Meanwhile, Erik remained faithful to another promise ~ to attend his cousin Ashley's wedding. Ashley helped care for Erik in the hospital during his excruciating spinal fusion surgery in which twelve inch rods were placed in his spine for stabilization purposes. The pain in the upper portion of his back where he still had feeling was so horrendous that Erik told Ashley to "keep it coming" even when he dozed off. She took some major heat from his nurse when she got caught doing just that with the Dilaudid drip button but she was faithful to her cousin. In return, he promised, "I'll be at your wedding." And apparently the Dilaudid didn't cloud his memory one bit; because less than five months later, he did exactly what he promised and drove five hundred miles, one way, to be there for her, at her wedding.

I was shocked that he made it. He was still healing from a shattered spine, various fractures, shredded lungs, and fresh surgical wounds from the long titanium rods that flanked each side of his spine; but he did it, with Jenny by his side. God, he looked like hell. He was so thin with grey skin tone and dark circles under his eyes, but he made it and I was comforted to see how Jenny stayed by his side. "She gets me," Erik said. And even though I believed that she got him, I wondered if she would continue to get him. I wondered if he would push her away. His controlled rage was palpable. I wondered if she could adjust to such a drastic change and completely different way of navigating life. But for a few hours that night, I let go of the worry and celebrated love. Admittedly, I did have an unspoken typical mom-moment. I had to scold my disappointed self when I noticed that Erik was wearing his favorite hand-me-down Chucktown hoodie instead of a dress shirt. "Really?" I scolded myself, "Like it matters what the hell he's wearing? He's alive! He's here! And Jenny is with him!"

Ashley's wedding was a milestone for all of us ~ one for her to celebrate marriage, one for Erik to prove his independence, and one for me to check my mom-moment at the door. I quietly admired my son's display of perseverance in the midst of his suffering. While my niece danced with her new husband, I danced with Chuck, my new dear husband of two weeks, and made a wedding wish for Erik and Jenny.

September 4, 2010
Erik with his cousin, Ashley
at her wedding

less than five months
after the crash

03 | pooping

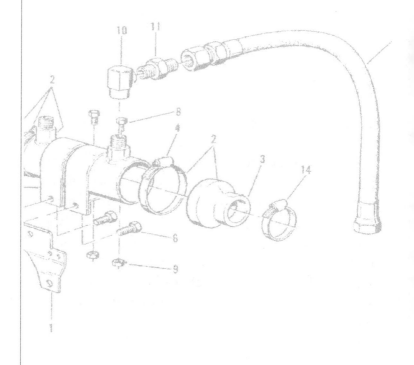

The week after Ashley's wedding, my dear friend Lori hosted a benefit for Erik in a suburb of Pittsburgh where I used to work. She'd always been my rock and this time was no exception. All I did was mention the word "benefit" and she took charge immediately. She personally planned and catered it, while still mourning deeply from the death of her eighteen-year-old son, Michael "Bubba" McGuire who'd been killed in the vehicular accident eleven months before Erik's motorcycle accident.

The day of the benefit, I watched Lori pull everything together but I knew she was an emotional train wreck waiting to happen. Lori's persona is larger than life so when her train jumps the track, it can be catastrophic. As the night went on, she started coming off the rails and it wasn't pretty. I held her hand firmly and quietly escorted her to the ladies' room. How could I possibly console my best friend, a mother who had lost her son while my son, although rendered paraplegic, was spared? There was absolutely nothing I could do for her but hold her hand while we sobbed together in a dingy little bathroom. If crying together counts for anything, Lori and I certainly had racked up our fair share of Frequent Crier Miles.

Grateful for the benefit, the support of friends and family, and proceeds of four thousand dollars, Erik insisted that we use the funds to obtain an attorney and get a patent for the idea we created to help him have bowel movements. The development of this gadget actually began in the rehab hospital where he was taught to wheel himself over a toilet on an open-seated toilet wheelchair after inserting a suppository, use his glove covered finger to stimulate his anus, and wait. I would look in the toilet to see if any stool had been evacuated.

If nothing came out he would eventually have to reach in the rectum and dig it out. It was humiliating and time consuming; he soon became infuriated with the indignity and inefficiency of that entire process.

One morning while Erik was still in the rehab hospital, after sitting over the toilet for almost an hour, he lost it and shouted, "That's it! Roll me into the shower ~ now!" I felt his anger and his embarrassment and shared those emotions with him. There had to be a better way. I rolled him into the shower and watched as he carefully balanced himself and placed the detachable shower head to his bottom. I thought he was washing his private areas. A few seconds later he took the shower head away from his bottom and it happened! Plop. Plop. Plop. His stool plopped onto the shower floor. I gasped. When he heard my response of guttural surprise he quickly asked, "Did it work?"

"You just pooped in the shower," I answered with curiosity. "Did you do that on purpose?"

"Yeah!" He replied with some excitement. "I think I can do this bowel program thing with water!" And he was right.

We never told the nurses or doctors what he was doing. He'd follow their bowel program orders and sit over the toilet, and as soon as they were gone I would roll him into the shower and he'd do his thing. Then I'd scoop up his stool from the shower floor using paper towels and flush it down the toilet. It was so quick and easy and clean ~ at least when compared to the rehab's method of bowel management. Erik's motivation for taking an even cleaner and more normal crap was heightened when Jenny insisted that he to move to her house straight from rehab.

"Pooping in your girlfriend's shower is not cool."

He shook his head in disgust for that unacceptable option. The short term plan for his arrival to Jenny's house was to use a bucket in the shower to collect the stool and then flush it down the toilet. But he wanted a way to complete the entire process while he was seated over the toilet. He wanted to poop like a normal person. Honestly, you never think about the convenience of pooping naturally until you can't do it.

The night Erik was released from rehab, we drove over three hours from the hospital directly to Jenny's house through a terrible thunderstorm. We had our own storm a' brewing ~ a brainstorm. During that drive we came up with an idea for a gadget that would mimic the shower bowel program he'd mastered in the hospital; only he would poop into the toilet instead of onto the shower floor. And although it wasn't able to be patented, the attorney felt the gadget had very real value. Obviously, we did too. Erik could poop fairly easy, while seated over the toilet, which is a huge deal. Bowel control was probably the most important obstacle to overcome, at least short term. Long term, there was a much more complicated obstacle to surmount, his ability to father his own children.

October arrived with stunning autumn color and was normally my favorite time of year but normal life wasn't anywhere in my sites yet. Nearly six months had passed since the accident and my head was still completely filled with thoughts of Erik, obsession combined with grief. I'd wake every morning from a restless sleep and as soon as I'd open my eyes, I'd think to myself, "My son opens his eyes and can't move. Every morning he wakes up to the same nightmare. How is he doing it? How is he coping? Oh God, please let him wake up from this nightmare." I had to do something on a daily basis to help interrupt my obsession. I'd thought about adding massage therapy as an additional tool in my bag of Intuitive Healing Coach modalities and decided that now, at age forty-seven, was as good a time as any to continue my education. Class would begin in three months. Until then, I knew had to do something else. I had to write.

I traveled to Harrisburg with my husband Chuck, where he was working at the time, and held up in a cheap little motel for an entire week to begin the cathartic process of writing the story of Erik's accident. Anyone who writes knows the power of the pen. I guess nowadays, we might say the power of the keyboard. That week I painstakingly revisited the entire accident from day one and put it in writing. Luckily, tears don't smudge a laptop keyboard, so I could cry without losing my work. I'd write. I'd cry. I'd write. I'd cry, and cry, and cry.

While I was writing and the tears were falling, I remembered a time years ago when my father gave me some sound advice. I was a teenager then and as often is the case with teenage girls, I was very upset about breaking up with a boyfriend. "Jacque," my father said, "you're going to be sad for a while. So I want you to take a walk up over the hill and bawl your eyes out. Take your good old time. When you think you're finished bawling, go ahead and cry some more. When you think you're finished again, make yourself cry even more. Cry 'til you can't. And when you can't make yourself cry anymore, come back down here to the house, get something to eat and go to bed. Then you get yourself up in the morning and live another day. It'll be okay."

Since I grew up on a remote farm in Pennsylvania, the hill was a good place for bawling; but so was a cheap little motel room. My father's wisdom remained sound even now. Tears help us heal. He knew that crying was good for the soul so he taught me to cry good and hard when I needed to. The dam of my own perceived strength crumbled and my tears flowed freely to the sea of tranquility. That week I completed a rough about the craziness of Erik's accident and miraculous survival, *Gratitude & Grit – A Mother's Healing Journey*, the prequel to this book. My path through grief was well underway but I couldn't even begin to imagine where Erik's path was taking him. I called him religiously every Sunday evening. I knew how hovering-mothering annoyed him so I refrained from calling more often.

He never answered his phone when I called. I didn't take it personally; he wouldn't answer anyone's calls. He completely secluded himself from everyone ~ except Jenny and the late-night internet video gamers.

So when my phone finally rang in late October and it was him, I was relieved to say the least. It had been weeks since I'd heard his voice. He told me that things were tough but that Jenny had picked him above everyone else. I sensed relief in his voice too. He didn't share a lot of details with me but obviously they'd been navigating their own tumultuous territory, deciding on what they could or couldn't handle for their future.

"No one's ever picked me before.

I'm going to make it worth her while.

I'm going to make it work and give her a good life."

I knew he meant what he said. I could tell by the tone of his voice. Statistically, the odds were stacked against them; but his odds of surviving the accident were less than zero and he beat them. Maybe the same spirit that got him into so much trouble when he was a boy was now working to his advantage. Just tell him he can't do something; then get out of his way and watch him do it.

04 | damn garbage

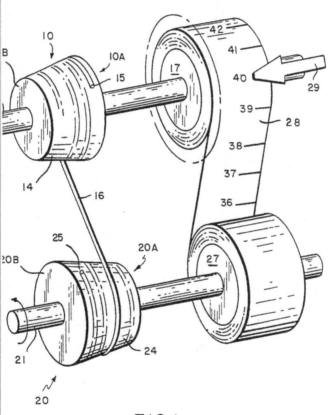

FIG. 1

aralyzed ~ saying the word was impossible at first. It took months for me to allow that word to be spoken from my lips. Eventually I began to accept the fact that Erik wasn't able to walk but I had a vengeance about him standing. I wanted to use the remaining funds from the benefit to purchase a standing wheelchair for him, but it just wasn't enough money. The spasms in his legs kept his muscles toned to some degree but the only way to maintain bone density in his legs was to bear weight on them, and that meant standing. When I'd push the topic he'd get snarky. "What's the use in standing when I can't walk anywhere?"

I remained relentless in spite of his attitude and continued to search for a way to get him to stand as soon as possible. I contacted his physical therapist who sent me a link to an online blueprint for a homemade standing frame which I promptly forward to my ex-husband, Erik's father, Ron.

Within a few days, Ron had constructed a standing frame from an old oak hutch that resembled a preacher's pulpit. It wasn't fancy but it worked. I received a picture on my cell phone of Erik standing in that frame on Thanksgiving Day at his father's house. It was crude but effective and since it was all we could afford, it would have to do. I was satisfied for now.

A few weeks later, Chuck and I went to spend Christmas with Erik and Jennifer. It was the first time I'd been back to their home since our fourteen weeks of post-accident togetherness. I figured that five months of separation was enough time for Erik but it was too long for me. I wanted to see him stand in person.

I'm sure that standing in a fixed position without the ability to walk only taunted Erik's rage but I hounded him anyway. I knew he'd want his legs to be as healthy as possible as he aged, especially if he had children. He just wasn't in the right frame of mind to realize it yet.

That was very tricky territory for me; it still is ~ knowing when to push and knowing when to back off. I remembered something a man at the garage told me when we were having Erik's hand controls installed. He was an older, wiser man who was waiting for his mobility van to be repaired. He talked with me quietly when Erik was out of earshot and said, "Let him come to you. He will, eventually. But let him be the one to come to you."

I didn't visit often, but when I did, I'd ask him to stand in the frame until he'd finally comply. Then I'd massage his occasional leg spasms while he stood reading a motorcycle magazine to pass the time. I knew darn well that he wasn't standing on a regular basis so I was shocked at his ability to stand for long periods of time. More than likely it was his determination to prove me wrong that enabled his lengthy standing sessions although I have to admit he does have remarkable genetics. He insisted that it wasn't important for him to stand. What was important to him was having a child and a family with Jennifer.

For months on end, Erik's world consisted of gaming on his computer all night and sleeping away the rest of the day on the couch; so when my annual trip to Cabo San Lucas rolled around that winter, I was chomping at the bit to take him. Erik had never been there and while he was in ICU, teetering between life and death, I whispered a promise in his ear. "You can't die yet. We have to go fishing in Cabo."

Knowing that a whimsical bribe wouldn't be enough to keep Erik from dying, I still had to taunt his unconscious brain, much almost as if to say, "I double dare you to live." Nine months after I made that promise, we were on our way to Mexico and I was very grateful to pay back that debt.

I wanted so badly for him and Jenny to have a great vacation. But I was really nervous about traveling and especially horrified about the possibility of a bowel or bladder accident on the airplane. There was no reason for me to think that would happen. He'd been accident free since the diarrhea incident when he detoxed cold-turkey from the pain meds seven months ago; but the unknown always rears its ugly head to invite anxiety right in the front door.

I corresponded with management at the resort to request a toilet and shower chair and insisted they measure all the doorways in the condo for wheelchair clearance. I even packed his bowel program so once we got there he'd be able to have regular and quick bowel movements during the entire vacation and not have to worry about accidents. I tried to think of every little detail to make the trip as convenient as possible for him.

Inconvenience for a paralyzed person is much more than inconvenient. It's a real killjoy. When everything you want to do is a hassle, life is a hassle and seems much less worth living. Until you're paralyzed, you can't know that.

~

We arrived at the open air gate in Mexico without a hitch ~ no bowel or bladder accidents. In fact, Erik catheterized himself in the seat of the airplane so discretely that no one even noticed. Once on the ground, the airline employees carried him down the plane's exit stairs in a tiny little airline wheelchair and he waited on the tarmac for his own wheelchair to arrive from baggage attendees.

The escapade of flying from North Carolina to Baja Mexico went much easier than I expected but even once we landed I still had some Mother Hen issues. Erik promptly nipped that in the bud during his transfer from the shuttle van to his wheelchair at the car rental office. It was a tricky transfer, high to low and quite a distance to traverse; so when I saw him start to lose his balance and take a nose dive I gasped and tried to help him. He made a valiant recovery and landed in his wheelchair but not without barking at me, "Damn it woman. Back off!"

Well, let me tell you, I backed off alright. As we waited in awkward silence for Chuck to arrive with the rental van, I kept my distance. Like a scorned puppy chewing on a bone of contention, I was waiting for my opportunity to bark back. Erik had become quite adept at putting me in my place while simultaneously tripping my trigger but I had become just as skilled at finding the perfect comeback. I didn't wait long until Erik dropped a gum wrapper on the sidewalk and said, "Mom, put that in the garbage for me." I was delighted that my opportunity had presented itself so quickly.

"Put it in the damn garbage yourself!"

I continued my sarcastic scowling. "You just screamed at me a few minutes ago when you could have simply told me that you were okay, so do it yourself, you little brat. You didn't need help to keep from smashing your face on the sidewalk while you were transferring out of the shuttle van; you surely don't need help putting your garbage in the trash can."

He grinned, seemingly content that he'd pissed me off and decapitated Mother Hen. Then he picked up the gum wrapper and put it in the garbage himself. The bell had rung. Everyone returned to their respective corners. The boundaries were in place. A fabulous vacation had just begun.

The second evening in Cabo, Erik announced during dinner that he had asked Jennifer to marry him the night before while they were strolling around, or should I say "rolling" around the resort. He looked like a smiling Cheshire cat as we waited for the answer.

| *She said, "Yes!"* |

We celebrated with hearts full of joy and my cup overflowed. It was another major milestone for their relationship and continued hope that Erik would rebuild his life with the help of this very special young lady. We truly loved Jenny like a daughter and could not have been any happier. They spent that entire week just having plain old fun. The kind of fun Erik used to have.

Erik had been an excellent swimmer since he was a small child and now even without the use of his lower body he was still able to maneuver very well in the water. It helped normalize the feeling of paralysis; it was where he felt the most comfortable. So he and Jenny spent a lot of time mingling at the numerous resort pools. He even challenged one little fellow to an underwater race and since Erik could only propel himself by the use of his arms, the race with a seven-year-old boy was very competitive and close. Erik barely won.

It had been quite a long time since he'd swum underwater and his once astoundingly strong lungs had been compromised not only from years of smoking but from the shredding sustained in his motorcycle accident and the surgery that ensued. Nonetheless, he surfaced in victory, gasping for air, grinning from ear to ear.

It was proof enough for me that Erik might be down but he certainly wasn't out. He could still hold his own in the water and have some fun in the process. When he and Jenny weren't at the pool they were fishing, swimming with dolphins, fishing, parasailing, fishing, bartering with locals for wares, and did I mention fishing?

My promised chartered fishing excursion started in the same way as getting Erik ready for school when he was a small boy. He was his normal ornery self at five o'clock in the morning. Nearly impossible to wake, he took his good old time getting ready. The more you push Erik, the more he digs his feet in. I was frustrated as we arrived to our chartered boat a little late but Erik, of course, was grinning smugly.

The boat mates lifted Erik's entire wheelchair on board, with Erik in it. Then he transferred to the boat's fishing chair and we secured him with ratchet straps that we'd purchased at Cabo's Walmart the day before. They weren't the optimal stabilizing solution but we hoped they'd be good enough to hold him in place and provide him with the necessary leverage to reel in a big one.

We were out about an hour before he finally got a hit. We grabbed our cameras and buzzed with excitement; he'd landed a nice sized Dorado and the ratchet straps worked. Erik had enough leverage and held his own during the struggle with the thrashing Dorado.

We were all enjoying the battle, rooting for Erik to emerge victorious. Then bam! Like an unsuspecting scene from a horror movie, something hurled out of the ocean, attacking the hooked Dorado while Erik was battling to reel it in!

As the story goes, a crafty old sea lion had been waiting and watching for the opportunity to snag an easy breakfast. It was a terribly gory scene. Blood squirted in the air as the sea lion leaped from the water to clamp the Dorado in its jaws and then plunged back into the water with its booty in tow. We were freaking out!

Now it was a battle between Erik and the sea lion, each fighting for the hooked Dorado. After a short tug of war, Erik reeled in the remains of the Dorado ~ just a beautiful severed head and proof that "the one that got away" wasn't just another big fish tale.

February 2011

Erik in Cabo with his severed Dorado head

Thankfully, my concerns for convenience were unwarranted. The layout of our resort was completely handicap accessible and its perfect location made it easy for Erik to access the marina. Even in town, wheelchair navigation was fairly manageable.

If there was a curb too big to hop, the locals were more than helpful. In fact, when the long steep incline uphill to the resort became too much for Erik to roll and Jenny to push, they just asked a local to help and paid five dollars for the favor. It was absolutely wonderful to see him engage in life again. As for me and Chuck, we lounged in the sun most of the time while Chuck serenaded me with his acoustic guitar and I studied anatomy. My forty-seven year old brain strained to memorize all the muscles, bones and their respective attachments sites as I crammed for a massage therapy test that awaited me when we returned from vacation. I'd peek up from my books to see Erik and Jenny rolling off on another adventure. It was almost normal. I could see a sparkle in his eyes again ~ an appreciation for life and that it was worth living.

After seven days, the time of departure was upon us and to put it mildly, Erik was absolutely miserable. He had such a good time, he didn't want to go back to his handicapped life and although he didn't exactly say it, he let all of us know it with his cranked-off attitude. We promised him that he and Jenny could use the condo again, for a honeymoon gift. It didn't alter his mood much but he held onto that promise as we returned to the States.

When we landed in North Carolina, Chuck and I went to retrieve the van while Erik and Jenny waited inside the airport for us to pick them up. While they waited, a lovely woman that Chuck had been chatting with on the airplane stopped and asked them to give us a bottle of wine that she'd brought back with her from her trip to Napa Valley. When we picked them up curbside and they gave it to us, I asked, "How did she know you were with us? We weren't all seated together on the plane."

"Really Mom, how could she miss us? You in your white fashion sweat suit and movie star hair, rock star Chuck in his dark shades carrying a shiny silver guitar case, tall white honkey me in my glow-in-the-dark white wheelchair, and beautiful little Jenny looking like my Hopsing sidekick! God! How could you possibly miss that circus parading through an airport?"

I guess we were quite a sight, but at the same time, our odd little family and Erik's paralysis were becoming more ordinary to me with each passing day. I was almost beginning to believe that life could be *normal* again someday.

I just hoped and prayed that Erik and Jenny's time together in Mexico would be enough to get them through the next phase of healing and building their life together.

*February 2011
Our hard-to-miss
traveling circus
boarding the
plane in Cabo*

05 | purgatory

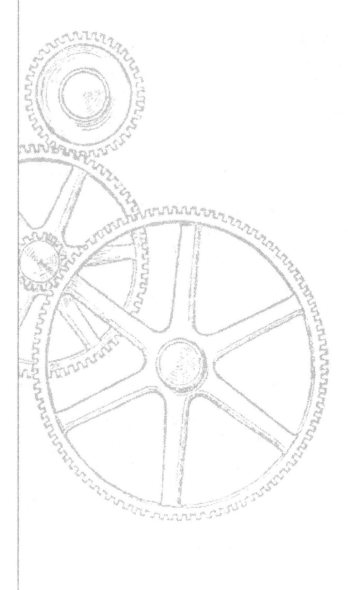

J was immersed in massage therapy school as the first anniversary date of the Erik's accident rolled around. My studies kept me from dwelling on the sadness of that unforgettable day. I did, however, excuse myself from class to say a prayer of gratitude and send a text to Erik at precisely 11:11 ~ a time and numerical symbol that we both hold dear.

> **Thank you for fighting for your life**

I didn't know it at the time but he'd canceled his cell phone service so he never received that text; probably just as well. He didn't need a reminder of that dreadful day. A cell phone bill didn't fit into his monthly income of seven hundred dollars, the combined disability and social security benefit I was grateful he received. Obviously, I was worried about him financially, but I knew he was able to live on a shoestring because he was raised that way. The lack of money would fuel his creative mind and ingenuity. Considering Erik only needed one drawer full of clothing, his necessary expenses were narrowed down to food and shelter. If he lived within his means, he had just enough money to meet his basic needs.

Frugality is a rare lifestyle these days but it's a lifestyle that I believe in, one that fosters character and humility; one that I believed would help teach Erik and Jenny the importance of faith, hope and love in the midst of a culture that wants it all right now.

When he called and told me they wanted to try in vitro insemination via a testicular biopsy, I was concerned about the cost. I wasn't able to help them financially. And even if I could have, I had a gut feeling that this fertility specialist was not the answer. Their desperation to have their own biological family made them vulnerable to expensive medical procedures that provided no guarantee of a child.

I was leery, to say the least. I encouraged him to be patient and felt sure that in time they would be able to have a child together without having to go this route. To be honest, I just didn't trust the medical advice they were given from the specialist with whom they met. He completely dismissed the possible option of electroejaculation stimulation ~ a method talked about in paralyzed forums and publications ~ the method Erik and Jenny hoped to learn about from The Miami Project. They still had not heard from the folks in Miami so they were desperate and in my opinion, that made them easy targets for exploitation.

The one thing that Erik and Jenny wanted so badly, a family of their own, was riddled by two major obstacles. He was paralyzed and he was broke. Because reportedly, no one else was involved in his accident, his basic motorcycle liability insurance provided no benefits. He had been laid off from his job at a metal fabrication shop the week before his accident and since he was obviously unavailable for work now, his unemployment claim was denied.

As Erik puts it, there was no golden parachute. It took months for the minimum disability benefit to kick in, which was greatly appreciated and extremely helpful, but it wouldn't even begin to scratch the surface of the cost that would be involved with testicular biopsies and in vitro.

Regardless of his helpless financial situation, Erik was up against the wall. Jenny wanted a child or else and the heat was on. It had just been a little over a year since the accident and Erik was still struggling with his paralysis. He wasn't fully engaged in life yet and remained unreceptive to any suggestions anyone would make to encourage him. But Jennifer had a way of getting the best out of Erik so I never questioned her ultimatums regarding a child. It was exactly what he needed. She fought fire with fire. All I could do was support them emotionally when they decided to use her credit card to finance an attempt at conception using a local fertility specialist via a testicular biopsy and in vitro process.

Sadly, within a few weeks they found themselves in debt and in doubt of ever having a family. The in vitro attempt was unsuccessful. Even though I didn't believe this doctor's advice was the best option for them, I did believe in the learning process of their choice. Erik in particular paid very close attention to the actual process of the in vitro procedure. He sucked it up like a sponge, making detailed notes in his determined mind, storing it all in his brain files for future access.

So even though they were devastated by the unsuccessful attempt which ended in a very early miscarriage, he hadn't given up. The gears in his head were turning. As summer lingered, the heat got hotter, both from the sun and from Jenny's ultimatum. They were stewing in the desire to have a family and Erik set his sights on trying to get a sperm sample on their own.

In the meantime, Chuck and I decided to sell our two-story home near Pittsburgh, Pennsylvania, because its only bathroom was upstairs. We knew that Erik would never visit if we couldn't accommodate him so we bought a one-level, fixer-upper near the town of Bradford, about three hours north. We began the necessary renovations to make it completely wheelchair accessible and worked there on weekends until I graduated from massage school at the end of June.

Then we immediately left Pittsburgh to continue remodeling and accepted a gracious offer to stay with our dear friends until our renovations were complete. Their home was nearby and provided us a home-away-from-home, a place to get a hot shower and a good night's rest so we could start work the next day feeling refreshed. While we were staying with our friends, the phone rang in the middle of the night waking me from a deep sleep. Thinking the worst, I scrambled out of bed, fumbling in the dark for my cell phone but when I finally located it, the ringing had stopped.

"Uh oh," I thought, "something must be wrong." I anxiously listened to the voice mail. It was Erik. He was rambling on and I couldn't understand anything other than "I know it's late but call me!"

He didn't have a cell phone anymore but he did have a Magic Jack internet phone line. I called immediately. My heart was racing. I knew he was alive, but my adrenaline was rushing when I dialed his number. I tried to speak in a whisper so as not to wake Chuck or our friends who were temporarily housing us.

"Mom?" he answered.

"Erik, is everything alright?" I whispered in a panic.

"Yeah, yeah! Everything's great! Okay, so I just had an ejaculation. It was brown but it came out! I've been fooling around with this special vibrator and it worked. Something came out! Mom, we want a child so badly and this is progress. We have to make this work." He was elated.

We talked for an hour, in the middle of the night, about next steps and not giving up. For the first time since his accident, I actually heard hope in his voice. It was exactly what he and Jenny needed. It wasn't a solution to their problem yet. But as he said, it was progress ~ just enough progress to help them hold on to hope and to their relationship; or at least I thought so.

A month later when Chuck and I visited, Erik was somewhat despondent. There had been no more progress with sperm retrieval and the strain was showing. The house was in complete disarray; Erik wasn't interested in anything but gaming on the computer. I was beyond concerned. I was mad. I kept my cool and held my tongue for as long as I could but just before we ended our visit, I lost it.

I curtly reminded him of a phone call he made to me and how he told me that Jenny had picked him over everyone, even family. I repeated his words back to him, quoting him, "No one's ever picked me before. I'm going to make it worth her while. I'm going to make it work and give her a good life."

"Remember that conversation?" I asked him, as the level of my voice raised, competing with my emotions. "Remember that? So just how are you making it worth Jenny's while? How are you giving her a good life? The house is a mess. You're home while she is at work and you don't even tidy the house or have supper ready? You think she likes coming home to a mess and to you playing games on the computer? There's more to life than the computer and the couch, Erik. You said you'd make it worth her while. That's not what I'm seeing! I can't believe what I'm seeing!"

My spewing continued with orchestral intensity. "You're better than this! Jenny is better than this! It's time to get your shit together and live again. Take care of this house! Respect your girlfriend's needs! Appreciate her generosity and start to live again; not play on a computer all night and sleep on a couch all day! I want you back, Erik. I want you back!" I was seething. Chuck quickly intervened by placing his hand on my shoulder and interrupted my livid rant.

"Erik," he said softly. "Your mother just wants you to be happy. We know it's difficult but we know you can do better. And we want to see you and Jenny happy together."

I was frustrated with Chuck for softening my message but the tenderness in his voice plucked some heartstrings. Both Erik and I started to cry. As Chuck and I walked to the front door to leave, I leaned over to kiss Erik and hugged him goodbye. He had stopped crying; his facial expression was cold and empty.

"I love you so much, Erik. I really do." The Erik I knew was gone. Tears rolled down my cheeks.

"I know. I love you too," he replied robotically. His detached demeanor kept me from feeling anything that even resembled love.

His words were as
cold and empty
as the look in his eyes.

It was purgatory.

Chuck leaned to hug Erik. "Love ya, brother," he said before he walked slowly to the car. I followed, wiping my tears and catching my breath between sobs. As we pulled out of the driveway, I looked at Erik sitting in that wheelchair on the front porch and my heart crumbled. I knew he needed a tough wake-up call but I also saw a broken young man on that porch, a young man that I gave birth to and loved more than life itself. I continued to sob out of control as we drove away. "I can't leave like this," my voice quivered with tears. "I can't leave him like this ~ not like this, not this way."

Chuck understood. "Let's go get some lunch and bring some back for him." That's my Chuckles. He knows nothing says I love you like burgers and fries. We picked up a greasy drive-thru feast and returned to find Erik still sitting on the front porch exactly where we left him, smoking a cigarette. Chuck handed him the fast food bag. "Hey Erik, we thought you might like some lunch."

I sheepishly chimed in, "And I couldn't stand leaving you this way." Big gumdrop tears plopped out of my eyes again. "I don't want to be mean to you Erik. I can't even begin to pretend that I know what you're going through. I'm so sorry. "

"I know, Mom. It's okay." He reached up to hug me.

It was **a real hug** this time and **I felt the love in it.**

I fell to my knees and laid my head on his lap. "I'm so sorry Erik, not for what I said. I meant it. But I am sorry for you. I'm so sorry you have to go through this. I love you. I love you so much." My voice trailed off as I buried my head in his lap to muffle my sobs.

"I know, Mom." He put his hand on my head. "It's okay. I love you too." Who ever knew the power of love wrapped up in a burger and fries? Chuck knew.

06 swimmers

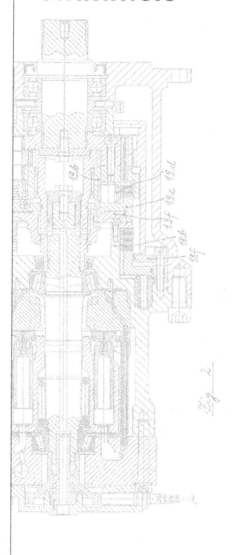

*I*t was late August when Chuck and I returned from the burger and fries meltdown. We'd barely been home a month when we received jaw-dropping news. Purgatory had passed. The Miami Project to Cure Paralysis finally contacted Jennifer.

Apparently, there had been a change in their staff about a year before; the same time Jenny submitted the online application. Erik's application to participate in their Male Fertility Research Program had been overlooked in the transition but was now being reviewed with great interest. Erik and Jennifer were invited to participate in their program, just like that. They finally caught the break they needed to try for a family of their own. They'd gone from purgatory to the front gates of Heaven in a matter of a few moments.

Travel plans from North Carolina to Florida were immediate. Erik was revved up and ready to roll. He picked up his father in Wilmington and drove to Miami, bunking in the nearby Motel 6 to be readily available for daily tests at the Male Fertility Research Program facility just across the street. The research team needed to gather specific information on Erik such as bone density, lung capacity and general health statistics that pertain to paraplegic fertility issues.

Jenny traveled by plane a few days later and joined Erik in Miami to be present for yet another attempt at in vitro. This time, if all went well, the procedure would be done using Erik's own mature semen and this time it would not cost thousands of dollars.

The Miami Project used electroejaculation, a semen extraction method that has been used successfully for years in men with spinal cord injuries, a method developed for animal husbandry. The procedure involved insertion of an electrical probe in the rectum. When electrical current is applied to the probe, the prostate is stimulated. It then contracts and ejaculates semen from the vas deferens of the male reproductive system.

Farmers and ranchers have done it for years with all types of livestock. Having grown up on a farm, I had no reason to believe it wouldn't work. We're all mammals with the same biological mechanisms and even though it might sound a bit unnerving, Erik has no feeling from the waist down; so all he had to do was overcome the perception of being rectally electrocuted.

I know my son. He was born a risk-taker and relentlessly driven to overcome his fears. The ultimate fear was death and, for him, that was an acceptable outcome of risky behavior. But paralysis was never considered as an outcome. I knew Erik could have willed himself to die or taken measures to do so after the motorcycle crash. The fact that he didn't give up was a true testament to his courage.

So, while it may have been unnerving to think about being electrocuted with a probe inserted into his rectum, it was nothing in comparison to the risks he'd taken in the past. This risk had new meaning. The potential outcome was the complete opposite of death.

| *The potential outcome was new life.* |

With no guarantees
of what his future
would look like,

Erik chose to keep fighting
through the torture of
paralysis and the loss of a
lifestyle he loved,

**because he loved
something else now ~**

he loved **Jennifer.**

Now he was taking risks to benefit someone other than himself. He was taking risks to benefit Jennifer and give her the family they both so desperately wanted.

The actual process of retrieving Erik's sperm via electrostimulation was successful on the first attempt. Erik's father telephoned me shortly after the procedure. He said he knew the sperm extraction was successfully because he could see a big smile appear on Jenny's face as she watched the procedure while Erik was behind a privacy curtain.

The urologist, Dr. Emad Ibrahim and Sonny Aballa, his assistant collected Erik's semen sample and analyzed it for sperm count and motility in the adjacent lab. They were as excited as Erik when they made the announcement.

"We got swimmers! We got a good one!"

They wasted no time and allowed Erik to immediately artificially inseminate Jenny with sperm from that sample on September 19th, 2011. It had only been seventeen months since Erik's crash, but it seemed like an eternity to them. Considering the paralysis factor, it was actually a very short period of time; but time lost, day by day, sitting in a wheelchair becomes purgatory. It's torture when you're watching time pass by until it slowly becomes your enemy.

It seemed that Erik and Jenny were finally gaining ground and the enemy was beginning to retreat. One year's time ~ one year's grief and heartache ~ had served as alchemy to their souls, strengthening their resolve and their relationship.

They made the most of their time in Florida and drove to the Keys for a few days of fun in the sun. The ocean, Erik's favorite place to be, was now a haven to do things that didn't require the use of his lower body. Water equalized him as much as anything could. He handled a jet ski quite nicely with Jenny as his passenger.

*September 2011
Erik and Jenny's first
Jet Ski fun together*

When they sent me this photo I caught a glimpse of the Erik I longed for. He was still alive in there, under the bondage of paralysis, the Erik I knew was still alive after all.

07 | aghast

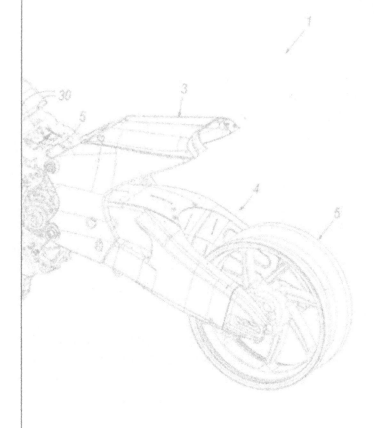

*W*ithin a few week of returning home from Miami it was clear that Jenny wasn't pregnant. Even though Erik's sperm extraction was a huge success, the insemination wasn't; Jenny felt that it wasn't optimally timed for her ovulation and she knew from her previous experience with in vitro that timing is everything. The Male Fertility Research staff invited them to return "anytime" and try again. Participants in their clinical studies are not charged any fees but are responsible for their own travel, lodging and meal expenses. With maxed credit cards and a budget that was already bursting at the seams, it wasn't a feasible short term option.

Jenny took it the hardest, thinking the worst, that it was hopeless. She was looking for a reason to keep believing in their dream of a biological family. Erik, on the other hand, was very encouraged and gave her every reason to keep believing. Although he was frustrated with the failed attempts and felt the immense pressure of creating a family like a ton of bricks on his shoulders, the successful electrostimulation sperm retrieval in Miami had actually renewed his hope for having a family and energized his efforts. He decided that if the Miami Project could retrieve his perfectly healthy swimmers, so could he. All he had to do was find the right equipment, hope he could use a credit card to purchase it, and then repeat the exact same process that was done in Miami.

The only difference would be that he'd be doing it by himself, to himself, at home. The mental notes he'd taken during each and every step of all the various procedures were etched in his memory. Risky? Maybe. But Erik was genetically coded to handle it. He did his best work when risk was involved. A lot of things changed for Erik when he became paralyzed but not his tenacity. Just tell him he can't do something then get out of his way and watch him do it ~ or watch him die trying.

~

While Erik was busy in North Carolina, surfing the internet in search of an electrostimulation machine, I was back in Pennsylvania. One day, I received a curious voice mail. I returned the call and spoke with a woman I'd never met before by the name of Katie. Her son Zac had been critically injured in a car accident and had sustained severe brain trauma along with other injuries and was not expected to live. She and her husband Ken were holding vigil by his bedside ~ in the very same ICU Trauma Unit that I held vigil over my own son just two years prior. The same nurses that cared for my son Erik were also caring for their son Zac and suggested that Katie and Ken read my book, *Gratitude & Grit*, which shared the intimate experience of my son's tragedy and his miraculous recovery in that ICU.

Katie said, "I can't even begin to tell you how much your book is helping us get through this ordeal. It's so much easier when you can relate firsthand with someone who has been through it." The book that began as a healing exercise for me had a niche purpose to help others with similar tragedies; to offer them encouragement and hope; to remind them not to give up.

My prayer alter was covered with prayers for Zac and his family. I sent love, light, Reiki and healing energy to them on a daily basis. It took many weeks but Zac pulled through and was eventually moved to the same rehab hospital as Erik. We shared a situational bond and promised to visit them during our next trip to North Carolina.

~

Back at the ranch of Erik and the conception desperados, extensive internet searches resulted in a successful roundup of an electrostimulation machine used for collecting sperm samples from goats. It wasn't exactly like the one used in Miami but both Erik and Jenny decided it was worth a try. I've got to hand it to him. I don't know many guys that would do what my son was about to do.

Erik and Jenny turned their bedroom into a makeshift conception laboratory. They had all the gadgets you would find in a gynecologist's office along with all the medical paraphernalia you would find in a fertility specialist's office. Everything was laid out on a night stand along with one other very special gift from a woman named Marilyn, Erik's massage therapist when he was in the hospital recovering from the crash. She gave him a beautiful ceramic trivet inscribed with a bible verse. That trivet had been on the nightstand since the day Erik moved to Jennifer's house. I read it every time I visited and remembered the special role that Marilyn played in Erik's healing process. She gave him the gift to remind him that his survival wasn't by chance and she was certain he had something big to share with the world. Now that trivet shared space with the equipment and supplies that Erik would use to attempt experimental child conception and now its message was more than profound:

For I know the plans
I have for you,
declares the Lord,

plans to prosper you and
not to harm you,

plans to give you hope
and a future.

~Jeremiah 29:11

Ovulation time had arrived. Erik and Jenny were all ready to get their experiment underway except for one small thing. He still needed to get sterile saline solution to wash the sperm sample before he introduced it into Jenny's body. So off to Walmart they went.

While Jenny went about her usual shopping, Erik rolled straight to the pharmacy. You can imagine the look on the pharmacist's face and his response when Erik told him he needed a supply of sterile saline solution and then proceeded to explain how he intended to use it.

"You're going to do what?"

The pharmacist was aghast.

"You're going to extract your own sperm sample using an electrical probe in your rectum, then wash that sperm with sterile saline solution and use it to artificially inseminate your girlfriend by yourself, at home?"

"Yeah, that's right," Erik replied like he was ordering a burger and fries at the drive thru window.

The pharmacist stammered. "Oh my, well we don't sell sterile saline solution, per say, but we do sell a baby nebulizer which includes a supply of sterile saline solution."

It was a perfect solution, no pun intended. "Great!" Erik replied. "I'll take it and be on my way." Soon Erik was on his way ~ his way home and his way to an experimental attempt at child conception, by himself, with no medical assistance.

08 a glimpse

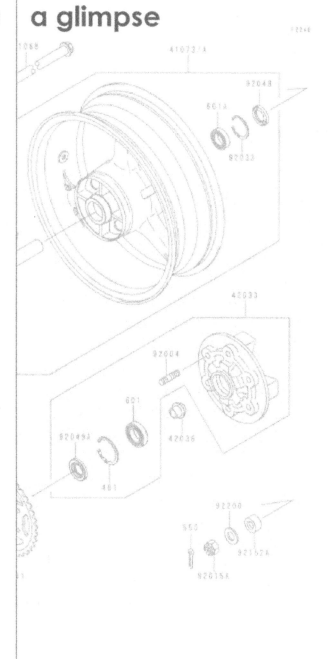

*E*rik and Jenny's first attempt at conception using the goat machine had us waiting with bated breath. I limited my questions, but seriously, how many moms had sons who were going to attempt an unconventional experiment like this? Considering the results of it could be my first grandchild, how could I not have an inquiring mind? There was a short lived moment of excitement when they thought the first pregnancy strip tested positive. But within a few weeks they knew she was not pregnant ~ again.

It was another failure as far as Jenny was concerned and she was growing weary of the heartache that accompanied each failed attempt. As Erik realized the extent of Jenny's disappointment, he began to get a glimpse of the impossibility of his experiment actually succeeding. He sounded sad; tired of trying and failing; tired of being tired.

Since the holidays were just around the corner, we decided to surprise Erik and Jenny with a deck that would look out into their backyard. Chuck and I coordinated with Erik's dad, Ron to work together on a joint Christmas present. The proposed deck would give them some additional outdoor living space and a nice place for Erik to grill outdoors, rather than in his garage. The day we arrived, Ron met us in the driveway. I was unpleasantly shocked to see a large wolf dog attached to Erik's wheelchair by a long leash.

"What the heck?" I thought to myself. "Don't tell me he got a dog?" I said nothing out loud.

"What do you think of that?" Ron asked enthusiastically as we got out of the car.

"Ah, whose dog is it?" I was hoping for an answer other than the one he gave me.

"It's Erik's dog, now!" Ugh. That's what I was afraid of. Ron proceeded to tell the story of how his daughter, Erik's step sister had found this beautiful dog with no tags wandering around at a gas station in Wilmington and decided to take it home. She called the pound and the police. No one had reported a missing dog. She put up posters. No one responded so she decided to keep it in her apartment, until the day they encountered a Chihuahua in the corridor of the apartment complex. The wolf dog pounced on the little dog and unfortunately, the little Chihuahua didn't survive the attack. Horrified and traumatized, Erik's stepsister called Ron to come and get the wolf dog. And that's just what he did. Then he drove straight to Erik's house to give the wolf dog another chance, with Erik as the new caretaker.

As I listened, my mind slowly rewound to a time two years prior when I was in Todos Santos, Mexico and captivated by a cutoff tree stump that had been carved to reflect the image of Christ's face. The owner of the boutique in which it was displayed called it her miracle piece because there was a new twig with bright green healthy leaves sprouting from the freestanding carved stump. I was so taken with the stump that I knelt in front of it to pray. Of course Chuck snapped some pictures as I was praying. He always seemed to interrupt my most private moments with that damn camera. But I have to admit, as usual I was glad he did because when I showed the pictures to a Shaman, she saw images in the carving ~ a medicine woman standing over a very sick man wrapped in blankets, a Reiki symbol, and a trinity of wolves' faces.

According to her shamanic reading tradition it was all part of a prophetic message for my life. A month later, Erik crashed his motorcycle. I stood over him for days on end, saying prayers, sending Reiki, and using essential oils as he was wrapped in blankets. Erik's middle name is Wolfgang and even though the nickname Wolfie never stuck, he loved to be called that and preferred his middle name over his first name. So I associated the symbol of the wolf trinity with his middle name.

But now a real wolf dog had appeared. My eyes popped out of my head and I looked at Chuck with a silent stare. He knew exactly what I was thinking. The shaman saw three wolves. This very large stray was clearly a wolf dog in my book; perhaps it was the second wolf in the trinity.

Erik named her Tika. She was an aggressive alpha female and her plan to dominate the pack was palpable. Her eyes screamed wild. Maybe that's what Erik liked about her. Maybe it would take a strong alpha wolf dog to challenge him and force him to engage in the daily tasks of life again. Maybe a pet would be the best thing for him now, although I'm not sure you would call this dog a pet.

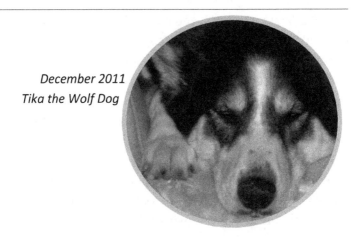

December 2011
Tika the Wolf Dog

We tied Tika to a metal stake in the yard so we could start construction on the deck but we may as well have tied her to a toothpick. She broke free in a matter of minutes so the deck project was immediately upgraded to include a fence around the backyard. Ron and Chuck worked together seamlessly as Father and Stepfather to complete the deck project without as much as a hiccup.

Erik and Jenny seemed pleased with their new outdoor space but their transparent grateful expressions couldn't hide the tension and frustration that was building. When Chuck and I were alone with Jenny in the car, shuttling for building supplies, we asked how she was doing.

"I'm doing okay," she answered quietly. "I just don't know about Erik though. He doesn't want to do anything. He doesn't want to go anywhere. It's hard for him I know. But it's hard for me too. I want him to engage in life again. When will he come back? Do you think he'll ever be able to?"

My stomach sank. This could be the beginning of the end of their relationship. They hadn't been able to conceive a child and the stress of an unplanned life with paralysis was building. Maybe it was too much for their relationship to withstand.

I shared with Jenny that most of the paraplegics I'd spoken with told me it took about two years to navigate the depression as well as adjust physically to their paralysis and begin to rebuild their lives. Erik would be hitting the two year mark in a few months. And truthfully, I just didn't know how long it would take because it's different for everyone.

I suggested couples therapy, specifically because of the traumatic experience of the accident and undoubtedly the profound impact it had on their lives.

Jennifer answered quietly again, "No, that's not how we work."

I heard and felt her words. That's not how they worked. Chuck and I were well aware that both Erik and Jenny marched to a different drum. We just hoped it was the same different drum. As we drove home with deck supplies, we assured Jenny that we understood her frustration and loved them both, no matter what happened.

Within a few hours Chuck and Ron were laying the last few decking boards. Erik was parked on the almost finished deck in his wheelchair using a hammer to sink the nails that weren't quite counter sunk from the nail gun frenzy that overcomes Ron when he is on a mission to finish a project. I was picking up pieces of scrap wood cuttings and cleaning up the work area in the yard. When I finished cleaning, I stepped up from the ground onto the new deck and scuffed Erik's closely shaven head. He looked up at me with such sad eyes. He didn't need to utter a word. His eyes said it all. But he spoke anyway.

"Mom, you don't know how badly I miss being able to do that."

He was referring to what I had just done, taken a step, one big step up from the yard to the deck. I used my legs without even a thought. I choked back my tears and looked into his eyes. They were different than they had been in the months following the accident. They were soft. They were humble. They were open to a different place. I no longer saw or felt purgatory.

Like the stranger we'd met
in the Goodwill store
many years ago,

**I could finally see deeply
into Erik's eyes,**
and

**I caught a
glimpse of humility,**

a glimpse of
Jesus.

It rendered me momentarily mute. No words would come out of my mouth. I just looked into his eyes, nodded my head, blinked back my tears, and acknowledged his sad, tired, beautiful soul.

"**Courage doesn't always roar.**

Sometimes courage
is the **little voice** at
the end of the day
that says,

'**I'll try again tomorrow.**' "

~ Mary Anne Radmacher

09 # shock and awe

*I*t was a long, cold winter for me and Chuck in Pennsylvania. It was a long cold winter for Erik and Jenny in North Carolina too, but a different long and a different cold. Pennsylvania's long and cold was snow and weather related. North Carolina's long and cold was related to Erik and Jenny's despair about having a biological family. The harsh reality was that their relationship depended on it. That winter Erik hunkered down and researched everything he could about at home in vitro while his wolf dog, Tika made one mess after another and demanded full life participation from Erik. Engaged in every realm, Erik was making real progress.

In January of 2012, they tried to get pregnant once more, using the goat electrostimulation machine to collect a viable sperm sample. In the privacy of their bedroom-turned-fertility lab, Erik inseminated Jennifer again and the initial at-home pregnancy test was positive. Excitement grew as those first days turned into two weeks, four weeks and still pregnant but Jenny began cramping at six weeks and had another miscarriage. We tried to reassure her that miscarriages were fairly common and it certainly was not an indication that she couldn't have a baby. Unfortunately, our efforts were no consolation to her. She was weary from the heartache that accompanied yet another failed pregnancy.

Erik on the other hand, had become a mad man on a mission. Though deeply saddened by the miscarriage, he was encouraged and recognized a very real possibility of success with his experiment. They had a pregnancy that actually lasted six weeks. He wasn't about to give up now. He continued to research ways to increase sperm and egg health and they both began taking supplements to support their reproductive health.

While he remained relentlessly focused on his conception quest, we decided to approach Vocational Rehab with a business plan to request assistive technology for Erik's garage so he could engage in his vocation and love of mechanics again.

As we worked long distance and prepared the business plan via telephone, Erik continued to search for electrostimulation machines. He needed a little more juice, aka voltage, than the goat machine generated in order to retrieve a better sperm sample. His persistence paid off once again. He secured a machine that was specifically designed to be used on bulls and was similar to the one used in Miami. As a descendant from a long lineage of farmers, I never imagined that the same animal husbandry techniques used by my grandfather on his dairy farm would be used by my son, on himself!

Maybe Erik was crazy?
Crazy or not, I trusted him.
More importantly,
so did Jenny.

I knew that if anyone could figure it out, Erik could. So I supported his endeavors while I held my breath just like I'd always done. Erik had been born a risk-taker so I decided early on that I'd rather support him than fight him; first, because I didn't want him taking risks behind my back, hoping I could mitigate any detrimental outcome with a sensible conversation; and second, because I've always sensed a special quality in Erik, one that drove his teachers crazy, but one that assured me he was not a quitter.

He was labeled as hyperactive in grade school and we were encouraged to medicate him to alter his behavior. Both his father and I dismissed that suggestion immediately. No doubt, Erik had always been a handful, but the spirit that exhausted us and drove his grade school teachers crazy was the very same spunk that had helped him survive his accident and endure the recovery process. Now it just might help him create a family. I totally believed in him ~ totally.

It was late March 2012. I drove to North Carolina to help Erik finish up his business plan for submission to Vocational Rehab with hopes that they would outfit his garage with the necessary assistive equipment for him to continue his mechanic vocation. It was a short visit of just a few days and before I headed back home to Pennsylvania, Erik and Jenny wanted massages and reiki treatments.

I'd done massage and healing touch with Erik many times before. But this time something unusual happened during his treatment. He was lying quietly prone on the massage table with my hands in the cranial sacral position when he suddenly inquired, "Mom, what the heck are you doing? My skull is on fire!" He didn't move. I didn't move either.

I opened my eyes and watched him closely as I spoke ever so gently, "I'm not doing anything but gently holding my hands on your sacrum and the base of your cranium while holding you in white light. Do you want me to stop?"

"No. No, don't stop. The fire is moving around the sides of my head and to the front of my face. This is so freaking weird but I'm okay." He took a deep breath. I held my hands gently in place and breathed deeply for a few more minutes until the burning in his skull and face subsided. When he was finally ready to get off of the table his legs were so relaxed they dangled like a school kid on a swing. Usually his legs were more rigid but something had definitely shifted.

Maybe a physical or etheric blockage had melted. Maybe the stored cellular trauma to his head that was sustained during the accident had been released. Truthfully, I don't really know. I don't have to know. I'm not sure I'm even supposed to know. I just have to believe that intuitive body work with the guidance of Christ's light heals.

Jenny had her massage treatment next and nearly fell asleep. She told me she had never been that relaxed before. A relaxed state of mind and body was a good thing for both of them and the baby-making process. My work there was done and I was homeward bound.

A week later it was show time ~ Erik's first attempt at retrieving a sperm sample using his newly acquired bull electrostimulation machine. It was the first time on record for someone to do electroejaculation at home and Erik had been advised by The Miami Project's Male Fertility Research staff of the possible risks involved since this procedure should only be performed by a trained physician.

"I have to admit," Erik reported when he called to tell us, "I was a little nervous, but I just went for it."

And the results were positive. He was able to collect a much better sample using the bull machine instead of the goat machine; of course, the bull machine generated more voltage, which also made the procedure even more dangerous. He washed his sample with the saline solution that he had retrieved from the pharmacist at Walmart then he carefully inseminated Jenny on April 7th, 2012. A sudden rush of goose bumps filled my body when I intuitively realized, "Oh my God. He's really going to make this happen." We didn't have to wait long for the good news to arrive.

| ***Jenny was pregnant ~ for real!*** |

The characteristics of **Erik's spirit** that once exhausted me now **stopped me in my tracks with shock and awe ~** electrical shock and awe!

I couldn't believe it had only been two years since the crash that rendered Erik paralyzed. In such a short period of time he and Jenny had accomplished something that had never been done before or at least had not been documented before according to The Miami Project to Cure Paralysis. Erik and Jenny had successfully achieved a normal pregnancy by themselves at home using animal husbandry techniques and artificial insemination. By Jenny's fourth month of pregnancy they told us that the baby was a girl. Wahoo! Yippee! A girl! Neither Chuck nor I had the experience of raising a daughter so we were absolutely elated at the idea of having a granddaughter due in late December.

Suddenly everything started falling into place. I self-published the book I'd been writing about the experience of Erik's accident, Gratitude & Grit - A Mother's Healing Journey, and it had begun to take on a life of its own. I realized that when that book was finally finished, I was finished ~ grieving that is, or perhaps vice versa. Maybe when I was finished grieving, the book was finished. Either way, the tears finally stopped falling. I was moving on. Acceptance of Erik's accident finally came to me as anticipation of what was coming filled the cracks of my broken heart.

10 | gizmo

Fig. 3

ith a new baby on the way and a self-published book to document the first part of Erik and Jenny's story, it was the perfect time to celebrate; so Chuck and I hosted a little party for them in Wilmington and invited all the folks who played a collective role in saving his life. It was an intimate open house gathering at a local pub and we managed to make it a surprise for Erik's 28th birthday.

From hospital staff and college professors to friends, family, and first responders, Erik and Jenny were surrounded by people that cared about them. A conversation with his teacher from Cape Fear Community College even prompted Erik to recover his old boat and begin renovations on it again; it was a sign of not giving up on his dreams. I sensed a surge of rejuvenation in him. After all, if he could make a baby, he could surely renovate his old boat, just like he'd renovated his life, piece by piece. Once he got back into the garage doing boat renovations, I could envision him fully engaged with his vocation of mechanics and enjoying his love for engine repair again, if the assistive equipment that he requested would be approved and installed by Vocational Rehab.

When Jenny reached her fifth month of pregnancy, Chuck and I sat down for a serious talk. "Okay, so now, this is real. Our first grandbaby is due in four months. We've got to get those kids a family vehicle." Chuck had been graciously recycling his old vehicles and giving them to Erik but they were cars, not vans.

Since Erik would be the primary caretaker when Jenny returned to work, we scrambled to find a used mobility van in our price range so that Erik could manage the baby by himself. We found a 1999 Dodge Grand Caravan near Pittsburgh, Pennsylvania. It was old but it looked to be in pretty good shape to us. Most importantly the controls for the ramp were the old mechanical style so I knew Erik could fiddle with them and keep it operating for a while.

The first time we watched him exit that van and roll down the ramp into Walmart's parking lot, his smile said it all. It was going to be a much better method of transportation for him, with and without babies. Erik's convenience to travel had been increased tenfold by having a mobility van; it wasn't quite as convenient as having mobility legs, but it's as convenient as it gets when you're paralyzed.

By October, the pregnancy was safe and secure but we hadn't heard anything from Vocational Rehab about the business plan that Erik had submitted six months earlier so I followed up personally. Unfortunately, there was a mix up. The paper work had been misplaced. I couldn't believe it. I insisted on speaking with the Vocational Rehab supervisor and we finally got to the bottom of it all; she took charge immediately and thanks to her, the long process of outfitting Erik's garage with assistive equipment was finally underway.

About the same time, Erik and Jenny begrudgingly began to recognize that their rescued wolf dog, Tika may not be the best pet to have around with a new baby. Tika had given them a run for their money, escaping whenever she could, mauling other little dogs in the neighborhood and dominating the household. She'd be a handful for any able-bodied person, let alone a paraplegic and a pregnant lady that weighed one hundred pounds soaking wet. They struggled with giving her up and asked if we could take her to my family's farm in Frogtown, Pennsylvania. I quickly ran that scenario through my head.

Let's see... **a farm with cattle, calves, cats, small dogs and children,**

mixed with an aggressive alpha wolf dog that has a rap sheet;

let's just say,

I knew it wouldn't be a pretty ending.

I made a few phone calls but the one that took care of it all was to my animal-lover cousin, who found a great home for Tika within fifteen minutes, in Pennsylvania. I assured Erik and Jenny that Tika would be fine and much happier in a cooler climate with winter snow. Reluctantly, they finally agreed.

They drove all night from North Carolina and rolled into Frogtown the morning before Thanksgiving. The van door opened, the ramp slid out and everyone emerged. The van's interior was filled with dog fur and the windows were covered with slobber. In her eighth month of pregnancy, Jenny looked like a petite China doll that swallowed a basketball. Erik had that look on his face, the one where one eyebrow is raised over piercing eyes. They were both exhausted, but before they went down for some sleep, he sternly warned us, "Keep Tika away from Gizmo."

No kidding. The last thing I needed was to have the little Shih Tzu that belonged to my brother and sister-in-law mauled. So I securely chained Tika to the heavy duty clothes line pole about twenty yards from their house, far enough away to keep Gizmo safe, or so I thought.

What I hadn't accounted for was Gizmo's friendly nature. When my sister-in-law walked down the lane to get her mail with her little Gizmo, he decided to leave her side and welcome the new wolf dog to Frogtown. We turned to look for Gizmo and by the time we saw him he was trotting happily toward the clothes line pole and his own demise. I sprinted to save little Gizmo from disaster but I didn't make it. By the time I reached them, Tika had Gizmo pinned to the ground with her mouth clenched around his tiny little body. Oh my God, I was frantic. I couldn't get Tika to release her grip on him. She had the power of a locomotive train fueled by alpha female instincts. I pulled on her collar, kicked and pounded her with all my might, screaming, "No, Tika! No, No!"

I knew I was taking a risk and could get caught in the cross fire of the attack but I couldn't stand by and watch her continue to snap little Gizmo back and forth. After what seemed like an eternity; but was only about ten seconds, Tika loosened her grip on Gizmo and dropped him from her jaws. Poor little Gizmo cried and whimpered and limped out of her reach before he collapsed. I remembered the story of how the Chihuahua died and I expected Gizmo to meet his maker right in front of us. I was sick.

Quickly, my sister-in-law Luanne scooped up her sweet little Gizmo and we ran to the house to put him in the bathroom sink where we washed and inspected his wounds. Gizmo had a puncture wound into his ribcage. I thought it was over, but he was still breathing and alive. We rushed him to the vet, poor little guy. He was in shock ~ very still and quiet on Luanne's lap while I drove, but still breathing and conscious. I was still breathing and conscious too, but I was as traumatized as poor little Gizmo. How do you ever make up for something like that? You don't.

Luckily, the puncture wound from Tika's canine tooth had missed Gizmo's lungs and albeit badly bruised, he survived the mauling. So we took poor little Gizmo home, all shaved, bandaged and medicated. When Erik awoke from his nap and learned about the nearly fatal incident he said, "I told you guys to keep her away from Gizmo!" Yes, he did. And no, somehow we didn't. And since farmers can't afford to tolerate that type of instinctual wolf dog behavior, Tika being chained to a clothes line pole on the farm wasn't necessarily the safest of places for her, if you know what I mean.

Even after the mauling fiasco, Erik and Jenny were still feeling bad about abandoning their rescue dog. My eyeballs popped out of my head. "You've got to be kidding me! If she does that to little dogs, what would she do to a little baby?" They didn't see it that way and insisted that she would never hurt a baby. I staunchly disagreed as we moved forward with the plan. That night, Thanksgiving Eve, the wolf dog, now a Frogtown farm fugitive, was loaded back into the van and delivered to her new caretakers. The guilt Erik and Jenny felt soon vanished when Tika got up and left Erik's side, ever so casually, and went directly to her new caretakers to lay at their feet as if to say, "Okay, I'm done with those people. You'll be my new pack now."

Tika had been spared, Gizmo had been spared, and Thanksgiving had been spared. Aside from Gizmo's bandaged body, it was a happy ending for all ~ happy enough anyway. If Tika had been the second wolf in the shaman's trinity, she had served her purpose and moved on to make room for the third wolf.

11 | hand of god

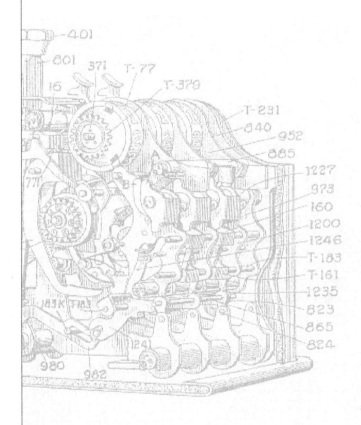

few weeks after the Thanksgiving episode, one of my wishes came true. Erik and Jenny got married on 12:12:12 at the magistrate's office near the historic courthouse in Graham, North Carolina with some random witnesses they met in the lobby. They wanted to be married before the baby arrived and since the due date of 12:28:12 was fast approaching, they found themselves standing in line with a lot of other couples who also wanted triple twelves as an official anniversary date. They finally got their turn and when Erik reached up to give Jenny a kiss during the proceedings the magistrate curtly interrupted him and said, "You can't kiss her yet! It's not time!"

Erik quickly retorted, "Have you seen her stomach? She's nine months pregnant. Don't you think I've already kissed her ma'am?" With that, their knot was legally tied.

On Christmas night, Chuck and I had just settled in for a long winter's nap at his mother's home in Pittsburgh. We planned to rise early the next morning, drive to North Carolina and stay at a hotel near Erik and Jenny for the remainder of the week, banking on Chuck's hunch that the baby would be born within the next few days. No sooner did we close our eyes when the phone rang. It was Erik. Jenny was in labor. It took me all of five minutes to be ready and waiting in the car. Merry Christmas! Our first grandbaby was almost ready to meet us.

Christmas also brought a winter storm. As Chuck carefully maneuvered snow and ice covered roads through the mountains of West Virginia, I reminisced in silence. Two years ago I'd made the same journey but under complete opposite circumstances; I wanted to make it to the hospital in time to say "goodbye" to my son before he died. Miraculously, he defied death ~ if for nothing else than for this moment, the birth of his daughter. Now I wanted to make it to the hospital in time to see him say "hello" to his own child.

I made it both times and witnessed my son choose life twice, once for himself and once for his child. Watching him deliver his first born from the seat of his wheelchair was a moment that exceeded my wildest dreams. I hadn't expected to be so involved with the whole event. I helped Jenny push during contractions with one hand and filmed the birth with my other hand while Jenny's mother massaged her daughter's legs and continually encouraged the pushing process. Guided by Erik's hands, the baby's head exited her mother's womb. I squealed like a school girl, "She's beautiful Jenny! She's beautiful!"

Erik and midwife Caron carefully removed the umbilical cord that was wrapped around the baby's neck then Jenny pushed once more and Erik escorted his tiny baby girl into this world. His hands claimed her immediately from the womb. He welcomed her with a tender kiss and basked in the glow of this miracle in his hands as he lifted her close to his face and said, "Hey there."

Suddenly, all the heartache was worth it. He had the most meaningful purpose possible and the most precious reason to live. They had the family they longed for;

| *Erik and Jenny had a family of their own.* |

Mila Mei Fugunt

6 pounds
19 inches

born December 26, 2012
at 11:01 AM

When Nurse Ann announced 11:01 as the birth time, Erik shot me a quick glossy-eyed glance with a big smile. I knew exactly what he was thinking and smiled back with silent recognition. Jenny's birthday falls on 11:11 and Erik was constantly seeing elevens when he began dating her just before his accident. Personally, 11:11 has been my favorite number since I was a little girl. Now Mila was born at the eleventh hour, the same hour of Erik's accident. Elevens are significant in numerical language and some folks interpret the sequence of elevens and zeros at Mila's birth time as follows:

Pay attention to your repetitive thoughts and ideas,

as they can be
answers to your prayers.

Do not focus on your fear.
God is talking to you.

If that doesn't sum it up, I don't know what does. We didn't need words. The numbers said it all. God was talking to us with a language felt by the heart, not with words heard by the brain. Besides, words could never come close to describing that moment in time. The miracle of birth is difficult enough to describe, let alone a birth with this backstory. There is absolutely no way my narrative could encompass it. It's like God. I can't describe God. I can only feel God. And God was with us.

With Erik's claim on baby Mila, I knew it would be a while until I could hold her so I immediately turned my focus to Jenny. After all, she did all the work. She had thrown up quite a bit during labor so I went into task mode. I immediately prepared a basin of warm water and cleaned her up. I got her something to drink and made her feel as comfortable as possible. Jenny was my daughter now and she would be treated as such. A family of their own equaled an extended family of my own.

Within the hour, all the family members had a turn at holding the baby, including me; but somehow a few minutes of coddle time just wasn't enough for me to wrap my head around what had just happened. Yes, I was excited. Yes, I was exhausted. Yes, I was happy ~ beyond happy. Even so, it was all surreal.

~

Once baby Mila was safe and sound at home, we drove three hours toward the coast for an impromptu visit to New Hanover Regional Medical Center in Wilmington, North Carolina. We wanted to make good on our promise to meet Katie and Ken ~ the folks whose son was in the same ICU that Erik had been in.

Their son, Zac was still in the rehab hospital, recovering from the tragic car accident in which he sustained severe brain trauma and physical injuries that impeded his ability to walk.

Before we made our way to find Zac, we made a quick stop at the ICU hoping to share the news of our granddaughter's arrival with the people that were instrumental in saving Erik's life ~ Bill Clark, who intubated Erik in the ER, and Louise "Weezie" Lanter, who cared for Erik in ICU. They had continued to follow Erik's progress long after he was released from their care, because they cared.

We lucked out. They just happened to be on call and we caught them in the hallway. Their efforts to save Erik's life weren't in vain after all and their concerns about his adjustment to paralysis were calmed. He'd made it through purgatory. We quickly shared baby pictures, tears and hugs then made our way to the adjacent rehab hospital.

My joyful exuberance of celebrating new life was abruptly hushed as we approached the hospital room that housed Erik during his rehabilitation. My chest tightened when we walked by the door to that room as sobering memories hit me like a tidal wave. I held my breath until we made it through that corridor. Then with each deep breath and each step forward, those horrible memories loosened their grip on my heart and we found our way to Zac's room.

Katie and Ken greeted us in the hallway and forewarned us of Zac's random, sometimes vulgar outbursts, explaining that it was a normal part of the neurological healing process. We couldn't care less. We were used to it. Erik's vulgar outbursts were random too, and part of his normal everyday neurological process! As we visited, I poignantly remembered what it felt like to be in their shoes, facing an unknown future with a severely injured son. And my soul recognized the element of faith that we all shared.

I deeply empathized with them, although I wasn't worried one bit about them. I knew they would make it through this. They had such spirit, spunk and most importantly, they had faith.

We kept our visit short and sweet. Chuck chatted away and talked music while I remained more reserved. I was more concerned about Zac's body and found an opportunity to gently touch his legs before we had to leave. As we bid them farewell, we hoped that our visit validated the hopes and dreams they held for Zac's future and we promised to keep in touch, all the while clueless that they actually held the key to a dream for Erik's future, which we would surprisingly discover in due time.

~

We started our journey home via a quick pit stop to say goodbye to little Mila, and when I say little, I mean little. She was just shy of six pounds at birth, so by the time she got home, she was only five and one half pounds. The love that filled Erik and Jenny's house made it easy to leave. It radiated peace. They were complete.

Hours later it hit me, as we exited the highway in Bradford, Pennsylvania; and it hit me hard. I had witnessed the miracle of Mila's birth and actively participated with tasks to do, but after a long quiet car ride home, my heart had time to feel it. Just five minutes from our snow covered driveway, far away from the surreal experience of Mila's birth, the entire event suddenly became very real and I began to sob. Chuck reached to gently hold my hand as gratitude filled me to the brim and overflowed in a river of tears from my eyes. I too, was complete.

I felt the hand of God,

the same hand of God

that I'd felt
at Erik's ICU bedside,

the unexplainable
presence of Love.

Apparently, I wasn't the only one who'd felt the hand of God along the way. Shortly after Mila's birth, I received the following messages from two ladies that I hardly knew:

Jacqueline,

Bless your heart... I want you to know that Erik's accident was a monumental incident in my life. You may think that I had something to do with saving Erik's life, but it was nothing I did. It was all God's grace. Erik does not know what an impact his life has had on my own. In a sense, Erik saved my life :) His accident started a cascade of incidents that changed my faith, spirituality, and ultimately my life. I am so happy that Erik has been able to receive all these gifts of love. His story is truly amazing. Congratulations on becoming a grandmother!

~ Linsey Elliot,

EMS First Responder

~

Jacqueline,

I just wanted to let you know, I met Erik with Jenny when they came to the hospital early on the morning of 12/26 after her water broke. I knew the moment I began interacting with them they were both special people. Ann, Jenny's delivery nurse, let me borrow the book, and after reading about your journey, I feel honored that I was able to meet Erik and Jenny. I witnessed a miracle.

~ Joy Wagoner,

Alamance Regional Hospital

12 take two

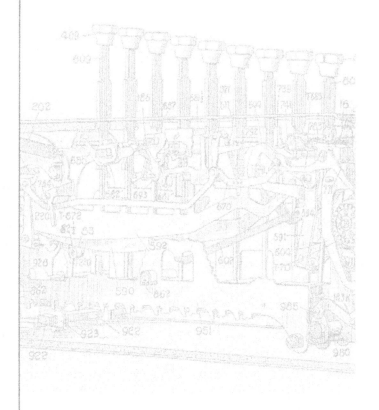

*E*rik and Jenny glowed with joyful contentment in their dream come true and quickly found their stride as Mila's doting parents; but the good fortune didn't stop there. Shortly after Mila's birth, Erik also rediscovered his stride as a grease monkey. Vocational Rehab finally came through for him. They approved his request and outfitted his garage with assistive equipment ~ a rolling tool cabinet, an overhead electric crane and a power standing wheelchair! Finally, Erik could work in the garage again, the place where he excelled. He was so excited and so grateful to the Vocational Rehab team for making it possible.

The power standing wheelchair was ideal for Erik's garage work. Its heavy motorized base stabilized him and kept him from falling forward while leaning over engines and lifting heavy parts. He could even use the work bench again and actually reach everything. I was thrilled to see how empowering it was for him, to do what he used to do and be independent in the garage. I wanted him to feel that sense of empowerment everywhere, not just in the garage; but the power standing wheelchair was too large and cumbersome for indoor use. In order to stand anywhere at any time, he'd need a lightweight manual standing wheelchair to replace his everyday wheelchair. I wasn't about to give up on that idea but for now, he could enjoy his incredible garage make-over.

Seeing him stand again meant the world to me and despite my concerns, he made it look easy, giving credit to the frequent leg spasms that had become part of his daily life. He refused to take any medication to reduce his spasticity and said the spasms gave his legs a workout. I guess he was right. All I knew is that standing was good for him and the precursor to walking again one day ~ somehow, someway, some day.

Meanwhile, Erik and Jenny adjusted to life with a new baby so flawlessly that they began trying for a second child immediately. Everyone thought they were crazy. Chuck and I already knew they were crazy so it didn't surprise us in the least. We were crazy too ~ over that new baby.

There was no way I was going to be a once-in-a-while kind of grandmother so I began making frequent solo drives from Pennsylvania to North Carolina to visit my new granddaughter. Fortunately, Chuck made the trip with me for Father's Day weekend and was given the ultimate Father's Day gift when Erik greeted us at the door with his infamous smirk and unexpected announcement.

| *"Well, we're pregnant again!"* |

Chuck and I laughed out loud as we shared in their joy. "What? No way! That's awesome! Oh my God, we can't believe it! You guys are crazy!" It was hard to believe; if he weren't my son, I may not have believed it. Erik inseminated Jenny in May of 2013, using the same animal husbandry techniques that he used to conceive Mila. This time they filmed the entire process for documentation purposes and once again, they successfully achieved a pregnancy.

Soon they would have two babies, just thirteen months apart ~ the first two documented babies born of pregnancies that resulted from an electroejacualtion procedure in which a paralyzed man collected his own semen and artificially inseminated his spouse at home, with no medical assistance.

Take Two!

Erik and Jenny

were making history,

making babies.

By late summer, we knew they were having a boy. Since Erik had talked about spinning his sperm sample to separate the males from the females, we thought he may have done so and used the male dominant sample to inseminate Jenny. But instead, they decided to let nature take its course ~ if you can call it that. The way they conceived children seem to take nature out of the equation.

Perhaps their decision to use unspun sperm was their way of adding the element of natural selection back into the equation. Regardless, this time around, the fastest swimmer was genetically coded with a Y chromosome. Nature had decided that Erik and Jenny needed a little boy to chase after, or watch after, their first-born little girl.

I turned fifty years old that July ~ a perfect age to embrace my role as grandmother. I was young and healthy enough to actively participate in a grandchild's life, yet old enough to wield some elderly experience and wisdom. It felt good. No, it felt great. Chuck and I even picked our own grandparent names for each other, JeeJee and ChaCha. Everything we'd been told about the glory of grandchildren was true. We were head-over-heels in happiness. It was hard to imagine anything interrupting our joy.

Two weeks before my birthday, I decided to get an early start on the last item on our home renovation project list; painting the interior of our garage. I was surprised to see Chuck, who was usually stuck inside his home office most of the day, wander out to where I was painting. I was concerned to see him taking a break so early in the day and was worried that he might be sick. "Honey, are you okay?" I asked as I stopped painting and watched him closely with a furrowed brow. A few seconds later he looked at me with glazed-over eyes and uttered the words,

| *"I just lost my job."* |

The tone of his voice reflected his total disbelief but it was true. Chuck had just received a phone call from the main office in Harrisburg. After a thirty year career in the insurance industry, he'd been let go without cause. It was a big hit. Understandably, he was in shock but it truly wasn't that big of a deal to me. I knew we could make ends meet somehow, no matter what it took. At least he had six months of unemployment compensation to help him process everything and review his options. Maybe now he could use his Physical Education degree from Slippery Rock University. Maybe he could finally realize the dream he had abandoned years ago and become a teacher.

Despite Chuck's uncertain employment status, we followed through with our plans to meet Erik, Jenny and baby Mila at Biltmore Estates in North Carolina for my 50th birthday present and we had a great time, as grandparents! Erik also shared with us an invitation he had received to attend the North Carolina Assistive Technology Conference in Concord, North Carolina. We all decided the opportunity was much too good to pass up but the conference was less than a month away; so as soon as we got home from my birthday excursion we made immediate travel plans back to North Carolina.

That's when the next big hit arrived. I learned that my work as a massage therapist with a local resort was being shared with another independent contractor, which meant that my already humble income would be compromised. I turned fifty years old and bam; the universe gave me one heck of an unexpected present ~ my husband and I were both facing uncertain employment situations. It turns out that losing jobs can be the best birthday gift ever; I just hadn't realized it yet.

With a bruised ego and confused heart, I decided to spend a day meandering about the spiritual community of Lilydale, New York to renew my spirit and gain some clarity. I found an anniversary gift for Chuck there as well, a statue of Ganesh. As Hindu tradition goes, Ganesh is a multi-armed man with an elephant head and embodies a divine force that quiets the rational mind and creates the faith to remove all obstacles and doubts. It was one of Chuck's favorites. When he'd seen it there before, he had picked it up and said, "Wouldn't this look nice on our mantel?" It was the perfect gift for him. But again, I hadn't even realized the pertinent symbolism that accompanied it, quite yet. When I gave Chuck the Ganesh statue as a third anniversary gift that evening, he loved it, of course; although it prompted a serious discussion about our situation and the need to create a game plan for our future. He wanted to stay in Pennsylvania, play music on weekends and return to school as a substitute teacher; then move south after a few years to be close to our grandbabies.

I was so excited about his decision to teach. His parents were both teachers; his mother taught art and his father, who had recently passed away, taught physical education. It was as though the teaching torch had been handed via divine intervention to Chuck. As he shared his plans, things suddenly became crystal clear to me. The sound of his voice resonated in my mind and I could see our future unveiled.

I said, "Why wait a few years? Let's move right now. We've been handed the perfect conditions to make the move, right now. We have a new granddaughter with a grandson on the way. Why wait? If we have to reboot our lives, let's just do it where we ultimately want to be ~ in North Carolina!" Flippantly I typed in a search for homes in North Carolina and a house right in Erik's neighborhood popped up, for sale.

I didn't need a brick
to fall on my head,
a statue of Ganesh, maybe
but not a brick!

Chuck was another story. He wasn't as enthusiastic when I showed him the house online. Reluctantly, he agreed to look at it when we went to North Carolina for the convention but he wasn't promising anything. He had a lot to digest; being unemployed for the first time in his life was not part of his game plan.

Chuck was an old college football player and a game plan freak. He knew if he moved to another state, his music career might take a big hit and he was passionate about that. It was a hobby but it meant the world to him and he had put too much time into creating a lifestyle that allowed him to use his talents. Not only was his love of music in jeopardy but he also had to break the news to his mother who lived in Pittsburgh and he knew how hard it would be for her if we moved so far away.

Chuck's talents extend far beyond music and he is instantly loved by almost everyone. I knew he could easily establish himself as a performer in North Carolina, but I wasn't sure how to solve the distance issue for his mother. I just pointed out to him that right now I was driving ten hours every six weeks to participate in the kids' lives and his commute to visit his mother in Pittsburgh would be three hours less. Since he hated the fact that I drove to North Carolina so often by myself, he seemed to have a change of heart and within a few weeks, he was on board with me for a new start in North Carolina.

His new game plan was exactly the same, to teach and resume his music career, but the playing field was in a different place; so he likened it to an "away" game and prepared himself emotionally for a change in venue. We put our house on the market immediately, figuring we'd have plenty of time to adjust to the idea of moving.

Erik needed time to adjust to the idea as well. When we told him and Jenny about our plans to move, Jenny was thrilled; Erik, not so much. Regardless, I found a few more houses in the area and made arrangements to see them all on the same day, when we would be there for the North Carolina Assistive Technology Convention.

We went, we saw, and looked at five houses and decided on the last house. It was perfect ~ about ten minutes from Erik so we'd all have our privacy. Before we made an offer, we wanted Erik to see it. He still wasn't thrilled about us moving there so he had an attitude from the start.

At the house, Erik insisted that Chuck wheel him up the front steps backwards. I was holding Mila so I couldn't help. Although Chuck didn't agree with Erik's idea, he eventually gave in. As he struggled to pull the wheelchair up the stairs, he accidentally dumped Erik out of the chair and on to the concrete sidewalk. Talk about a rough start; Erik's knee was badly scraped and he bled all over the front walk. Once he got back in the wheelchair, the realtor and Chuck lifted him and carried him into the house. When I put Mila on the floor of the master bedroom and she started to cry, I immediately picked her back up, which only infuriated her father even more.

"You're going to spoil her!" he growled at me. By the time we finished our walk-through of the house, I was ready to go. It was clear that Erik didn't want us there. We went back to his house and had a serious discussion to clear the air. Chuck, who had mastered the role of mediator, stood by to keep the peace. Slowly, Erik explained that he didn't want to hurt me; but he didn't want me taking over their lives. He wanted me to be like Poonie, my own mother, who always has a hug ready when you need it.

Ironically, that is what I thought was doing when I picked Mila up from the bedroom floor but as the conversation continued, I began to see that Erik's concerns went deeper than I realized. He had developed a high functioning style of fathering around his paralysis. He didn't want me to mess up his system, logistically or emotionally. He didn't want Mila to expect to be picked up immediately with every whimper because he physically couldn't do that and he didn't think it was good for her, even if he could.

Suddenly a light went on for me. He made being a full-time paraplegic father look easy but it was anything but easy. Mila had adapted to Erik's condition and it was crucial for me to respect that in every way. I also respected the fact that Erik needed his privacy and personally, I felt the same way.

A few years ago, after his accident I had moved into Jennifer's home as his caretaker, and had basically taken over. He didn't need or want that from me now. He just wanted me to be a grandma and to mind my own damn business.

I got it. And I knew I would have to be much more conscious of my overachieving personality and try to subdue the non-stop activity that accompanied it. At the end of the day, all was well. Good thing, too, because the very next day we would drive two hours to Concord to participate in the Assistive Technology Conference. Being stuck with each other at a conference for a few days could have been ugly if we hadn't cleared the air. A truce was in place and we were ready to roll, no pun intended.

13 still alive

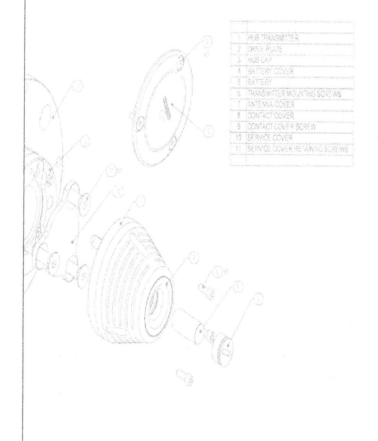

1	HUB TRANSMITTER
2	DRIVE PLATE
3	HUB CAP
4	BATTERY COVER
5	BATTERY
6	TRANSMITTER MOUNTING SCREWS
7	ANTENNA COVER
8	CONTACT COVER
9	CONTACT COVER SCREW
10	SERVICE COVER
11	SERVICE COVER RETAINING SCREWS

ince Chuck was seasoned with conference experience from his insurance career days, he attended the welcome dinner while Erik stayed in the hotel room and conducted a blog radio interview about his story.

The next day, with Chuck's lead, it didn't take long for Erik to get comfortable in the exhibit hall and make a little splash at the conference. It even led to his invitation as a guest speaker for the following year's Assistive Technology Conference. The staff from North Carolina's Vocational Rehabilitation program who helped facilitate the event were proud to have one of their own rehab clients actually participating.

As Mila's handler, I presented her for a late day cameo appearance and she immediately stole the show. Erik perched her on his lap and took a roll through the exhibit hall to show her off. The only thing missing was Jenny, who wasn't able to take off work. I hoped she could attend next year's conference. I wanted her to see how her commitment to Erik had helped him blossom into so much more.

That week, the offer we made on the house in Graham, North Carolina was accepted. At the same time we had multiple offers on our house in Pennsylvania. The ease and congruency of selling one house, while buying another and moving to another state, was almost unheard of.

Southern hospitality welcomed us kindly; the gentleman that sold us his house graciously built a garage entrance ramp for us so Erik would have easy access to the house and there wouldn't be any more blood spilled on the front walk. It was all said and done within eight weeks. That's when you know God is in the driver's seat and you better just hold on for the ride; but buckle your seat belt. As if there weren't enough wild rides in this story, it gets even better. On Sunday October 6th, 2013, we were traveling from Pennsylvania to North Carolina to close on our house in Graham and I got a call from Jenny. When I answered the phone she greeted me with, "Oh, I just had to tell somebody."

My heart skipped a beat. "What?" I asked anxiously. "Is everyone okay?"

"Yes, we're all okay. But Erik is at the hospital with someone else." Then she continued to tell a story that, quite honestly, sounded like a big fish tale. I listened intently with my eyebrow halfcocked in disbelief.

As it goes, Erik was working on an outboard boat engine in his garage late into the night. It was 4:30 a.m. when he finally finished up. The outboard engine that once sputtered and stalled was buzzing like a bee. I'm sure the neighbors appreciated that in the wee hours of morning. Anyway, he shut the engine down, removed his noise silencing head phones and rolled out the open garage door to throw away some trash. In those few seconds, across the silence of a crystal clear starry night, he heard it ~ the unmistakable sound of tragedy. A horrible crash peeled through the silent sky; wheels screeched, metal crashed and crunched, then nothing but eerie silence.

As a crash connoisseur, Erik surmised from the horrific sounds that a car had lost control, made impact with some permanent objects in the woods, then rolled over three or four times and came to a halt. Cushz … Quiet … Cushz … Quiet … Cushz … Silence. He listened intently a few more moments before he rolled into the dark house and woke Jenny who was five months pregnant. He told her what he'd heard and thought he should go investigate.

She agreed and waited at home as he began his search with the most logical route, Route 119, the most traveled road near his house. Heading south from Hawfield's Country Store, he drove slowly while carefully scanning the roadsides for two miles. There were no signs of an accident so he turned left onto a secondary road, Jim Minor Road, and continued to scan the roadsides for nearly another mile. As he approached a bridge and dangerous curve, he noticed that one of the arrow signs indicating a sharp bend was missing. He remembered there were usually three of those signs at that curve. Now there were only two.

He aimed his headlights into the woods but couldn't see any crashed car. What he could see was the missing arrow sign lying in the woods. So he got out of his van and rolled his wheelchair close to the berm of the road where he noticed fresh tire tracks going into the woods ~ tracks from a vehicle that had knocked the sign over. He yelled into the woods, "Hey, anyone there?"

The only reply that came from the wooded darkness was an eerie silence. Erik called out again, "Hey, is anyone in there? Flash your lights if you can hear me." Still, nothing. A few cars drove by but they didn't stop when Erik tried to flag them down.

Really?

How do you drive by

a guy in a wheelchair

that waves you down

at dawn's darkest hour?

The lack of concern from passersby didn't deter Erik's efforts in the least. He was determined to find the source of the crash that he'd heard peel through the night sky. He called out one more time to no avail before he made the five minute drive home for Jenny's help and cell phone. They left baby Mila at home with Jenny's parents, who just happened to be visiting for the weekend, then called 911 as they both returned to the suspicious crash site and waited for emergency responders to arrive. While they waited, Jenny used her cell phone flash light app to look into the woods and the creek that lay below. But still, they saw nothing more than the fresh tire tracks and the arrow sign that had been knocked over.

Soon a full convergence of first responders arrived but after a long unsuccessful search, the ambulance was released and left the scene. The responding officer in charge surmised that there had been an accident but that whoever had gone off the road must have driven away or had been towed out. Erik was not convinced. There was no indication whatsoever that a vehicle had been towed from the woods; there were no tire tracks exiting the woods, no disturbed ground ~ nothing. Less than fifteen minutes had passed from when Erik heard the accident until he found the site so there wasn't time for a tow truck to arrive and pull out a car. It seemed as though someone had lost control on the sharp curve, veered off the road, plowed over a road sign and then simply vanished.

Erik was furious that he couldn't use his legs to investigate on his own. He wanted to walk into the woods and down to the creek bed to see for himself. He continued to plead his case with the officer ~ that no one could possibly drive away from a crash as violent as the one he heard. His gut sense told him that someone was in there. The officer must have sensed Erik's frustration and for the sake of the persistent crazy guy in a wheelchair, he descended into the creek bed once again for another look. This time he shined his flashlight across the water to the opposite bank. That's when he noticed a few pieces of shimmering chrome, perhaps a possible site of impact ~ on the other side of the creek.

Realizing that maybe Erik wasn't crazy, he climbed back up from the creek bed and crossed the bridge where the entire emergency rescue crew had been standing for quite some time, then entered the woods on the other side of the creek. It wasn't long until the officer quickly emerged from the woods, waving his flashlight with urgency. He'd finally found something.

"Did you find him?"
Erik called out.

"Yeah!" the officer shouted back.

"Is he still alive?"
Erik called out again.

"Yeah, he's still alive!"

Now that the mystery of the vanishing car had been solved, they were able to retrace a path and confirm every sound Erik had heard. The car had lost control at the apex of the sharp curve, knocked over the arrow sign, veered into the woods, glanced the metal bridge abutment and became airborne, sailing over the creek. It then rolled bumper over bumper multiple times up the far side creek embankment and back down the other side before it came to rest in a dense thicket of foliage, completely hidden.

*Early morning
October 6, 2013*

*Actual scene of the vanished crash
Jim Minor Road, Alamance County*

*First responders standing on
the bridge looking down into
the creek; no car was visible*

*The yellow > arrow
sign was plowed
down and the car
flew airborne over
the creek below
landing hundreds of
feet away, in a dense,
dark thicket of woods*

Far from the curve where it first lost control, the car had landed on the driver's side with the roof of the car slammed against a tree, perfectly camouflaged and concealed from view. Rescuers jumped into action immediately and used chainsaws to rough-cut a clear path through the woods; then they carefully removed the driver from the car with the Jaws of Life.

As Erik watched
the rescue unfold,

his own gut-wrenching accident came flashing back.

He would've been dead if the same amount of time had passed before he'd been found. It had taken such a long time to locate this crash and extract the driver that he feared the worst. As the young man was carefully extracted from the crashed car and carried out of the woods, Erik surmised by the visible damage to the driver's left arm that he didn't survive from loss of blood. He somberly asked a second time if the driver was still alive and was surprised when the medic replied, "Yeah, he's alive, for now."

Erik wanted to know the driver's name and asked if they'd found any identification. Responders had found a wallet. "Brandon Jeffries," they replied. "He's twenty years old." Erik had seen the name "Jeffries" on a military style back pack which was retrieved from the car. It wasn't just a crash anymore. It had a name, Brandon Jeffries; now it was personal.

Erik and Jenny sat in the van and watched as the ambulance and all the first responders drove away. And just like that it was over, almost like it never happened. Jenny had seen a brilliant light above the tree line that night while they watched the rescue unfold. She said it must have been the light of Jesus. They sat in silence at the scene after everyone had gone and felt the unspeakable power of divine intervention.

Erik had experienced

this same tragic event
just three years ago,

except then,

he was the guy
they were struggling to save.

God had placed him on the rescuer's side this time. He took Jenny home and found the hospital where Brandon had been taken. He knew he had to go there; to follow up and answer the questions his family and friends would undoubtedly have. Someone had to tell them what just really happened.

Erik rolled into the UNC Chapel Hill ICU and saw a few people in the hallway, clearly in distress. "Are you with Brandon?" he asked, as he momentarily interrupted the grief stricken family trying to make sense of the tragic news they had just received.

They looked at this complete stranger in a wheelchair with puzzlement on their faces. "Yes, and who are you?"

Erik's vulgarity filter was non-existent. He'd been awake for over twenty-four hours and had just lived through and participated in the tragedy and suspense of a made-for-TV movie. His answer reflected his state of mind.

"I'm the guy

who found

the poor bastard."

Erik recounted the detailed story of Brandon's crash, pumped up with natural adrenaline and the artificial fix of Red Bull coursing through his veins. For the first time, through another family's grief, Erik experienced the anguish his own family felt the day of his accident. The realization sobered his Red Bull high. Brandon's mother, Gwen Jeffries, chronicled her son's healing journey and wrote the following excerpt in her journal about her first encounter with Erik at the hospital that morning.

In a state of shock…we sat, paced the floor and sat down again in a repetitive pattern of dismay. I decided to walk out into the hallway to check on Chris (my husband). He sat on the teal cushioned bench alongside his uncle, cousin and father. There was a young man in a wheelchair talking to them. Uncle Roger looked at me and said, "Gwen, this is the man who heard Brandon wreck."

Now, come on. Who hears a wreck at 4:30 AM? An Angel, that's who. I walked over and just gave him a hug. I wiped tears from my eyes as he recounted the moments that had transpired. As he finished telling me all he could, I saw the look of exhaustion on his face. He said he needed to get home and get some sleep. We exchanged phone numbers …and he was gone.

I couldn't believe what all had occurred and how our lives could be turned upside down in the blink of an eye. But one thing I did know. I was not afraid. I felt the presence of God with us. And he had no intention of leaving us anytime soon. Not to mention that I had met an earthy angel ~ his name is Erik.
He was sent to save my son's life.

Gwen Jeffries' 2013 journal entry

By the time Chuck and I arrived at Erik's house he was back home from the hospital, collapsed on the sofa, with Mila tucked close to his side, sleeping soundly in the protective arms of her daddy. Erik was too emotionally and physically exhausted to give us all the details but he shared a shorten version of the nightmare he just experienced. We listened in sheer belief, our jaws on the floor.

I couldn't help myself as I shamelessly probed him, "I'm just curious Erik, what if that was your little Mila or your son who will soon be born?" I wanted to know if his perspective on life and taking risks had changed now that he was a father.

Erik choked back his tears. He rubbed his eyes with the back of his hand, shook his head back and forth and uttered, "I couldn't do it. I can't even think about it." His voice quivered as his mind trailed off to join Mila in a sound sleep, the two of them stuck together like glue.

What a welcome to North Carolina. If that were any indication of what lie ahead for us, we should have known there'd never be a dull moment in our lives ~ ever again. Then again, considering Erik's birth date and the fireworks that had ensued ever since, part of me wasn't the least bit surprised by this unbelievable story.

Life was a new normal.

14 special powers

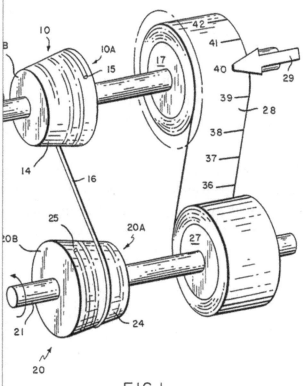

FIG.1

*E*rik and Jenny's plan to take us up on the Cabo honeymoon offer was cancelled as their trip fell during Jenny's final month of pregnancy. Since the timeshare would be empty, Chuck and I decided to go ahead with a little vacation and meet up there with some dear friends of ours from San Francisco.

We hoped like heck that unborn baby boy would stay in his mama's womb until his due date, which was a week after our scheduled return. Both Erik and Jenny kept telling us, "He's coming early. We can just tell." We wanted them to be wrong. But on Wednesday, February 5th, I received a text message.

At the hospital

Dang it! They were right. That little rascal was coming eleven days earlier than his due date with JeeJee and ChaCha hundreds of miles away, in another country! Grrrr….

A decision was made to induce labor because the baby was big enough, in place, and Jenny was dilated. Now all we could do was wait and wish we were there.

We didn't have to wait long for our second grandchild to arrive. Once again, Erik's choice to live, if for nothing else, was to deliver his second child ~ a son. When he called to tell us, his voice was like that of a childbirth veteran. With the help of midwife Angela, he'd delivered another child from the seat of his wheelchair and was as proud as any father could be.

"Well we have a

perfectly healthy baby boy

and mama did it all natural.

She did great,

but I'm still getting yelled at."

Apparently Jenny's decision to forego an epidural this time made her delivery very different from the first once. As any mother understands, she was pretty vocal about the pain and Erik, like most fathers, had to absorb the sound waves. I was so disappointed to be missing it all but Jenny had already diplomatically decided that it was only fair to allow different family members present to experience the birth.

Knowing that it wasn't my turn to be in the delivery room made it a little easier to be away, but I was counting every second for the next three days until we would be back home and I could see our new grandson, Wolfgang Tiberius Fugunt ~ perhaps the third wolf of the shaman trinity.

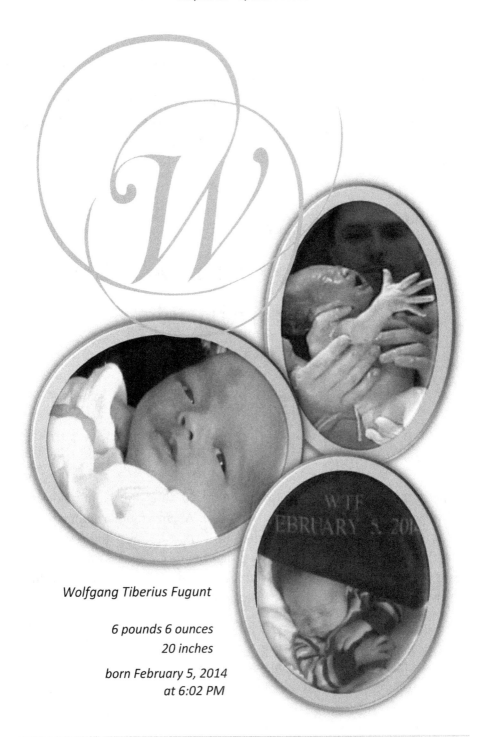

Wolfgang Tiberius Fugunt

6 pounds 6 ounces
20 inches

born February 5, 2014
at 6:02 PM

The next day I messaged the exhausted parents to request a picture of our new baby boy. I thought it was odd that I had to ask. And when a picture finally came through, it included a message that said baby Wolfie had some bruising on his face from delivery ~ okay, no big deal. In fact, the friends we were with in Mexico showed us a picture of their second child and he had extensive purple bruising on his face when he arrived to planet earth; it's not always an easy trip! But having that photo of Wolfgang's bruised face made me want to get home even more quickly. Our friends also loved our new grandson's initials and thought the acronym for the corresponding expletive was the appropriate response for this whole crazy story so they had a blanket embroidered for him with those initials ~ WTF ~ for Wolfgang Tiberius Fugunt.

Two days later we landed at the Charlotte airport on an evening flight. I'd missed a call from Erik and thought it was odd for him to be calling me that late at night but assured myself that he was just excited for us to meet our new grandson. I knew Chuck was tired but I insisted we see the new baby that very night so I returned Erik's call and asked if it would be okay if we stopped over, even if it was after midnight. "Yeah, sure, as long as you are not too tired. We'll be here, so whatever you want to do." His voice was calm and casual ~ too calm and too casual. Something was up. I told him we'd be there as soon as we could.

As we drove in silence I suddenly wondered if maybe the bruise on baby Wolfie's face wasn't a bruise. My tummy flipped in a rush of panic. I took a deep breath. "It'll be okay," I reassured myself silently. "It'll be okay," I repeated my affirmation. Then I closed my eyes, breathed and prayed.

When we got to their house, I held little Wolfie for the first time and his dreamy little body melted into my arms. He was much cozier to hold than his lightweight wiggly sister had been when she was born. As I held him, I studied his handsome little face.

His right eye was puffy and looked swelled. The purplish so-called bruising covered most of the right side of his face. After I finished adoring him, I finally asked as tactfully as possible, "Are you sure this mark on his face isn't a birth mark?"

The hesitation provided the definitive answer but was followed by a disconcerting explanation from Erik. "We didn't want you to worry while you were on vacation. First they told us it was bruising from delivery. Then we were told it was a Port-Wine stain which can be an indication of Sturge-Weber syndrome, a serious condition that in rare cases causes mental retardation, developmental delays and seizures."

The flip I had in my tummy during the drive home just flopped. Erik rolled from the living room to the kitchen. It was obvious that both he and Jenny were devastated and thinking the worst case scenario.

I handed our precious handsome baby grandson to Chuck and went to the kitchen to hug Erik. I assured him that everything would be okay. His eyes were full of dammed back tears and his voice quivered, "I can take the stain. Really, it's growing on me. In fact it's kind of cool, but I can't do Sturge-Weber. I just can't do it."

"Oh Erik," I hugged him. "It'll be okay. I promise. Wolfie will be okay. And so will you and Jenny. You're the perfect parents for him. You know what it's like to overcome adversity. You'll be his example. And you're right; the mark is kind of cool, like a natural X-Men mask! Maybe he'll have special powers too."

I shifted my delivery from sympathetic to tenderly jovial while trying to honor their deepest fears, all the while fascinated with the mark that formed a prominent Orthodox cross on Wolfgang's forehead. Talk about protection from evil; he was bodily anointed with the sign of Christ.

Erik answered with sudden conviction, "Yeah, he'll be a telepath." He was joking, but not really.

I think we both knew
right then and there

that Wolfgang
really would have
special powers.

Chuck and I comforted Erik and Jenny the best we could that night. I'm not sure we lightened their heavy hearts but they knew we were here to support them every step of the way. Now that we officially lived nearby, we could provide logistical support for any medical care that our beloved grandchildren required and we had plenty of time to offer, which was an upside of our present lack-of-employment situation.

On our way home, Chuck told me that he thought it was a birth stain from the first picture they'd sent but he didn't say anything. He recognized it because he had an uncle with a very similar mark and informed me that once he held Wolfie, he sensed there was no Sturge-Weber condition. Admittedly, Chuck has a special sense for those kind of things and assured me that our little grandson was just fine; but regardless of what Chuck sensed, I was still concerned. Once home, I set up my altar and healing stones with little Wolfie's hospital tee shirt. I started my faithful ritual of prayers and Reiki ~ light work for Wolfie, but also for Erik and Jenny to feel strength, love and support that would provide peace for them on this unknown path.

Erik and Jenny had taken Wolfie home from the hospital within twenty-four hours after his birth, refusing all shots and inoculations. They were adamant not to introduce any foreign substances into his tiny body until they knew for certain the extent of the Port-Wine stain condition. To make matters worse, a rare and severe ice storm hit North Carolina and shut down everything, including doctor's offices so referrals for Wolfie to visit various medical specialists had to wait.

Life had literally stopped. Roads and stores were closed. Even the power, electricity and heat, were gone. Erik and Jenny were forced to sit in the cold, huddled together under a blanket, keeping their family warm as though hiding in deep dark trenches waiting for danger to pass.

A week later, when the storm had passed and the ice eventually thawed, a referral was finally made for Wolfie to see an ophthalmologist to determine if the stain had compromised his eye sight. That appointment was four weeks away, which was completely unacceptable, so Erik decided to take matters into his own hands.

He packed up his precious family into the van and headed for Duke University Health System. He pulled up to the front door of the medical building and herded everyone into the ophthalmologist's office completely unannounced ~ ballsie, to say the least.

I'm sure their unexpected parade must have made quite an impression ~ Erik in his wheelchair, Jenny holding Wolfie and overwhelmed with fear that his eye might not be functioning normally and fourteen month old Mila, wobbling around the reception area, looking for trouble. Ballsie worked. They found themselves promptly seated in an exam room with the head of Duke's ophthalmology department who determined that Wolfie's eye showed no signs of visual impairment. The results of that wild ride calmed Jenny and Erik's hearts somewhat and they began to relax a little for the first time since little Wolfie made his debut.

Shortly after that, I got an unexpected visit from Erik ~ at midnight. He'd purchased some old speakers on Craig's List to outfit his living room with surround sound and he wanted to borrow our truck dolly to help transport them; it was a great project to alleviate some of his recent stress. I stood in the driveway while he sat in the van for over an hour. He didn't want to come in. After all it was just an impromptu visit to pick up the truck dolly ~ at midnight. The best talks always seemed to happen late at night.

After mostly idle chatter about the surround sound project which, he implied, would require my services to run wires in the crawlspace under his house; he admitted how scared he was for Wolfie and the potential Sturge-Weber syndrome condition. I acknowledged his concerns wholeheartedly and talked about the benefits of doing healing hands energy work. Erik was completely on board. He'd experienced those modalities firsthand. "I'm all for it. Do it," he said.

"You know I am doing it every time I hold him?" I told him and figured he already knew.

"Yeah, I know," he smiled.

"Do you pray?" I asked.

He smirked and scoffed. "No." But after a short pause he recanted. "Well, yes I did. I said, 'God, I don't ask for much, just this. So if you don't come through for me, when I get there, there's going to be hell to pay. And if I don't get there, I'll hunt you down.' " I chuckled as a big grin appeared on his face. That's not quite the kind of prayer I had in mind but at least he was communicating and acknowledging the power of God; and it was genuine. We talked more about how a parent's love is the most healing energy of all, a manifestation of God's love for mankind. God is the most pure form of energy and light. I assured Erik that he was a vessel of that light for his child.

"Yeah," he said. "I hold little Wolfie's head in my hands all the time." Erik had already been doing his own light work.

At six weeks, a dermatologist who specialized in Port-Wine stains for infants helped ease Erik and Jenny's fears even more. After examining Wolfgang, he felt the odds of Sturge-Weber were less than two percent and recommended pulsed dye laser treatments as soon as possible, confident that the stain would fade almost completely. I made a soft suggestion to spare the Orthodox cross on his forehead but was overruled; I loved that cross.

At ten weeks, Wolfie was finally seen by a neurologist. He checked out completely healthy. All that would be required right now was cosmetic treatment of the Port-Wine stain for a few years and periodic ophthalmology exams to monitor the health of his right eye. Although no signs of Sturge-Weber had been detected, symptoms of neurological and development issues can occur up to two years after birth; but we weren't going to focus on that. We were claiming Wolfgang's good health and moving on. It was one of those times I remembered my father's wisdom once again; something he told me twenty years prior. "Life just doesn't come with any guarantees, not for any of us. Do the best you can with what you have to work with. And keep looking forward."

The worry and panic melted from Erik and Jenny's faces with each visit to the doctor and with each breath thereafter. They finally began to enjoy their little guy without thinking every noise he made, or didn't make, was an indication of Sturge-Weber syndrome.

The birth of Erik's second child initiated a deeper awareness of God's grace and healing gifts. Erik always understood loving energy. Now I believed that he understood it at a much deeper and more personal level, as a life giving force which flowed through him; and he understood how it would help Wolfgang.

With a clean bill of health for her baby boy, Jenny's maternity leave would soon be over. She could return to work with a big sigh of relief and Erik could happily resume his role of full-time father in charge of baby boot camp.

Jennifer and Erik with their growing family

March 2014

It seemed as if everything was beginning to settle down, when I received this message from my Aunt Carol ~ the same aunt that was with me when I walked into Erik's ICU room for the first time after his accident; the aunt who acted so cool but later told me she thought she was going to pass out when we went into that ICU room. Yeah, real cool. Anyway, she sent this message.

You have to do this!

CALLING ALL HEROES – A LOCAL HERO CONTEST

Local Heroes all across the United States and Canada have been sharing their stories about how they or someone they know have overcome the challenges of living with a disability. Encourage your family, friends, and co-workers to vote for the Local Hero you think is most deserving to "Win a Custom Wheelchair Accessible Vehicle."

Wow! Well, the crash Erik heard in the middle of the night, that resulted in saving Brandon's life, was a hero's story if there ever was one and certainly worth a chance at winning a mobility van. The contest allowed a short written essay or a two minute video entry. If we could get Brandon's family involved with creating a home video, it just might make a pretty compelling entry.

15 | # glows in the dark

*J*ennifer had kept in touch with the Jeffries during Brandon's recovery. From what I gathered, Brandon had suffered substantial brain trauma in addition to the horrible damage to his arm which he had hanging out the window during the crash. He wasn't expected to walk again and although his recovery was slow, he was alive and healing, little by little.

I asked Jenny to contact Brandon's parents, Gwen and Chris, to see if they would be interested in shooting a home video for contest submission with Erik in his garage from where he heard the crash. They jumped at the opportunity, eager to show their appreciation for Erik's role in saving their son's life in any way they could and agreed to meet us at Erik and Jenny's house the following Saturday.

Erik had met Brandon's parents the night of the accident in the ICU, just six months earlier. The rest of us had never met until that Saturday afternoon. We were busy introducing ourselves and getting acquainted when Erik noticed someone walking towards him ~ someone he didn't recognize at first. It was Brandon, walking very slowly but nonetheless walking, towards Erik.

Caught completely by surprise, Erik reached to shake Brandon's hand and said, "Wow, I didn't expect to see you here. You're doing great. Walking, talking, everything! Good to meet you, man."

As soon as Brandon's mother Gwen and I saw each other, we hugged tightly and our embrace lasted until our tears stopped falling. We didn't even speak. No words were necessary. We shared the same story, the same heartache from tragedy, the same gratitude, the same spirit, and the same heart of a lioness mother.

Once again I was reminded of a very tender place ~ the early months of Erik's recovery and healing journey. I recognized that same place in Gwen's eyes and listened deeply as she shared some of their story.

We finally got around to shooting the home video. Erik and the Jeffries were nervous and Jenny doesn't like being on camera so it was as authentic as could be ~ unscripted, unrehearsed and uncut, but that video completely captured the essence of what had happened six months ago on that fateful night when Brandon crashed.

Brandon's father was filled with tearful emotion as he thanked Erik for saving his son's life and Brandon's mother praised Erik as going "above and beyond the call of duty". We named the home video after her sentiments and uploaded it to You Tube as our submission to the contest, *Erik Fugunt - Above and Beyond.*

If nothing else, it was a wonderful way to reunite two young men who shared and triumphed over tragedy, as well as those who loved them. I knew exactly how Brandon's family felt. I was feeling those same emotions when Erik crashed, about the people who didn't give up on him even after he died a few times. The gratitude one feels when their child's life is spared knows no boundaries.

| *It's an indebtedness that can*

never ever be repaid. |

That day I also learned that Gwen, Brandon's mom had the same worrisome apprehension that something was going to happen to her son, like the intuitive knowledge that I had about Erik; it was just another uncanny connection that Gwen and I shared.

Chris, Brandon, Lindsey, and Gwen Jeffries

Jennifer holding baby Wolfie ,
and Mila fidgeting on Erik's lap

The garage reunion
March 22, 2014

Brandon's mother Gwen and I worked together feverishly for the next month promoting the story and the contest. I was brand new to North Carolina so I had no contacts or connections anywhere. I literally started from scratch to uncover every stone for help. I even went door-to-door and stopped complete strangers on the street to ask for internet votes; somehow the word spread like wildfire.

It was covered by WFMY *News 2 Wants to Know* in Greensboro, featured on the front page of three local North Carolina newspapers, blogged on an NPR radio station website at UNC and featured in our old hometown Pennsylvania newspapers for the Pittsburgh and Clarion areas. The local Cinema in our new little hometown of Graham, North Carolina even donated a big screen promotion and ran it during their movie previews. Erik and Brandon's story was getting some press and votes from Facebook supporters were adding up.

When Erik stopped at Hawfield's General Store for his weekly visit, he joked with the clerk. "Hey, I need a pair of sunglasses. The paparazzi are driving by my house."

"Really?" the clerk, who was as big a tease as Erik, thought he was serious for a moment.

He grinned and she gave him a glaring sarcastic retort, "Well, you still gonna talk to us now that ya'll are famous and on the front page of the newspaper?" She had just as much vinegar in her humor as Erik did. And although he was having some fun with all the notoriety, he claimed all the while that he was just doing what every person should do when they hear a crash in the middle of the night; that he didn't put himself in harm's way so he really wasn't a hero. I reminded him that he tried to flag down two cars that drove by that night and they could have run him over, but he just laughed.

"They wouldn't have run me over.

My white wheelchair glows in the dark!"

In the midst of all the extensive interviews regarding the story of Brandon's accident and the van contest, Erik was unexpectedly contacted by the University of Kentucky's Frazier Rehabilitation Institute in Louisville. Supported by the Christopher & Dana Reeve Foundation, Frazier Rehab is having great success with experimental electrostimulation epidural implants for paralyzed people.

The four initial young men that have received the epidural implant from Frazier Rehab have regained some voluntary movement in their lower extremities. They have also experienced improvement in their bowel and bladder function as well as sexual function. Erik is in their database of interested participants for clinical trials so I'd been monitoring their progress closely via the foundation's website. They were calling to invite Erik to participate in a study, but for the external electrostimulation and not the epidural implant.

I was beside myself with excitement. Erik was calm, collected and torn. He'd love to participate but he couldn't reconcile the fact that he'd be away from his family for four months, all expenses not paid, for an external stimulation study when what he really wanted was to receive the epidural implant. He carefully considered his options and financial resources and hugged Jenny tightly. So much was happening so quickly, but Erik kept a cool head.

I knew he wouldn't accept an invitation to participate in Frazier's study unless it was for the epidural implant. I was concerned that if he turned down this opportunity, they would never consider him as an implant candidate; but his priorities had changed drastically since he became a father. His family was his priority now, taking rank over himself and his ability to walk. His children came first. They were his life. His decision was to pass on the external study and hope that he would one day be called for the epidural implant. I couldn't argue with that. And even if I wanted to, we didn't have time. We had to get on the road for a TV interview that would air live on the 5:30 early evening news!

When we arrived at the studio, Erik chatted candidly with Tanya Rivera, an anchor with WFMY News 2, in Greensboro and told her that he would try to refrain from using his normal colorful language as he smirked,

---

"I'll try not to cuss on live TV.

Sometimes it just come out,

kinda like Tourette's."

Ms. Rivera's face suddenly paled with serious concern. "Oh, maybe this isn't a good idea." She'd never met Erik before. As far as she knew, she could potentially be lighting a loose cannon on live TV.

I gave her a reassuring look and gave him the stink eye. "He'll be fine. He does not have Tourette's and he knows when to hold his tongue. However, he does like to tease relentlessly, which is what he's doing to you right now." She grinned and took a deep breath; her body language showed her relief.

We met the Jeffries at the TV station. When Brandon arrived he was as white as a ghost. He still suffered with severe motion sickness from his brain trauma medications but he pulled himself together and those two young men interviewed splendidly. With the help of a very skilled anchor person, the live airing with Erik, Brandon, and Brandon's mother Gwen, was a success! And not a moment too soon, as far as Erik's van was concerned. The 1999 van we'd found for Erik a few years ago was starting to require a lot more maintenance.

The van was cosmetically intact and had no engine trouble when we delivered it to North Carolina from Pennsylvania. But once Erik inspected it a little more closely he found crushed glass in hard to see places, evidence to support that the van had previously been wrecked. Even though the automated ramp wasn't working quite right, he was able to get it working better. It was his first official mobility vehicle and once he got over the stigma of being a young guy in a minivan, he became very attached to it. As the months passed the van began having other issues. The air bag suspension system developed a leak.

So Erik's father did what he does best. He started rigging. He removed the airbags and flipped the rear axle, then mounted the van body directly to the axle with no suspension or kneeling option. One disaster averted. At least the van was still operable.

Then the driver's side window fell out. Then the rear passenger window fell out. Erik had the driver's window replaced but just plopped the rear passenger window back in and gave strict orders never to open it again. He was stranded at one point because the key would not start the ignition. After dismantling the steering column, he discovered if he hammered on the ignition it would start. So he just kept a hammer in the vehicle as his backup starter. The rumbling exhaust needed repaired; the paint was peeling off the rusted rear wheel well; but most recently and concerning, the motor that operated the sliding door and ramp began to fail. I crossed my fingers and hoped that it would hold up until Erik won the new van.

Meanwhile Chuck had been working the music scene, securing gigs and making new friends when he heard about William Earl Mace, a well-known and beloved local musician. Mace had suffered a severe stroke that rendered him hemiplegic, paralyzed on his left side. When we attended a Sunday afternoon benefit in his honor, Mace made an honorary appearance. It was the first time he'd been out of the hospital in four months.

When we learned how he arrived at the benefit, laying on his back in the trunk area of a borrowed non-handicap accessible van, we immediately offered to borrow Erik's handicap accessible van to transport him back to the rehab facility in Durham from the benefit in Greensboro.

That was the first time we met Mace and even though Erik's challenged van had seen better days, for Mace, it was better than the alternative. At this point neither Mace nor his girlfriend had any means of transportation, at all. Her car had just blown up a few days before.

After we delivered Mace safe and sound to the rehab facility we returned the van to Erik and gave him the low down. When he heard Mace's story he said,

---

"If I win a new van,

I'll give my old one to those guys,

as is, because it needs work,

but it runs.

It's better than nothing

and right now they have nothing.

I know what it's like."

Once word spread about Erik's gesture to pass it forward, the contest vote count increased significantly from an average of one hundred-fifty votes each day to nearly four hundred votes daily. With that push, Erik secured enough votes to become a semifinalist in the van contest. We'd done our best. Now it would be up to a panel of judges to decide which four contestants from over one thousand entries would win a new mobility van.

16 family bonds

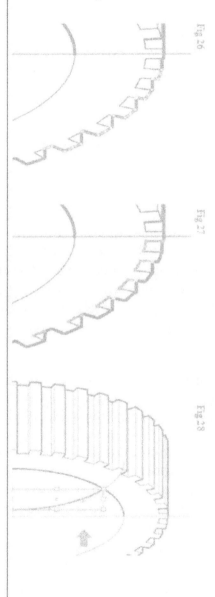

We were elated, and so were Mace's friends. Erik's 10,297 internet votes were enough to qualify him as a semifinalist in the van contest. If Erik wins, Mace wins. And even though Mace's prize would require some tender loving care it was better than his current arrangement of an ambulance service for transportation.

The two weeks of waiting with anticipation for the judges to choose the winners were much easier than the anxiety-riddled weeks of campaigning for internet votes. I was at peace. We had done everything humanly possible to give Erik a chance to win a new mobility vehicle.

By this time, Chuck and I had been married three years. The impromptu move to North Carolina was a whole new adventure for both of us. We were in a strange land, meeting new people, making new friends, searching for work, finding our way. Believe me, creating an authentic life together, from scratch, in your fifties is not for the faint of heart. I remained true to my massage therapy vocation and Chuck took on the challenge of substitute teaching while staying true to his love of music by securing local gigs. "Home Team," he'd say with a fist bump. It was a reassuring gesture, especially when our savings began to dwindle.

Chuck was my Home Team. Our marriage was the second time around for both of us. We knew it wouldn't be easy to start over again but we'd made it this far and we certainly weren't about to give up now; the adversities we'd experienced together thus far had only served to strengthen our relationship. And besides, we were starting over again with new life ~ two precious grandbabies. We'd made a decision to relocate based on our hopes to foster close family ties with our grandchildren and there was no turning back. We had to hang tough and make it work.

The family bonds
we'd both craved for so long
were beginning
to take root,

with Erik and Jenny
and even more so

with Mila and Wolfgang.

I guess Erik was beginning to feel some Home Team too. He asked if he could store his salvaged motorcycle in Chuck's garage ~ the same motorcycle that he was riding when he crashed and became paralyzed. I took that as a sign that he trusted us with a very important piece of his life. That motorcycle held huge significance for Erik and what he loved to do. It didn't remind him of being paralyzed. Neither did the helmet he was wearing that fateful day, which he now displays in their curio as an icon of his assumed infallible youth.

~

May 30th arrived ~ the day we would find out if Erik won a new mobility van. His story was so amazing and so unique; it seemed impossible that he could not win. We felt it within our hearts so deeply that both Chuck and I could even see it in our minds. When we talked about what color it was; we both came up with the same vision ~ a dark blue van.

As always, though, the fine print seems to dampen the spirit of the game. I discovered that the winner would receive an IRS 1099 form and have to claim the van as "taxable" income. The idea of coming up with funds to pay the tax was more than a little concerning; I was beginning to panic about how we would be able to come up with that kind of money. But on the day I expected to be notified that Erik had won the van, I got the shock of my life. We never received a phone call. We never received an email. Erik didn't win. I couldn't believe it. I was literally dumbfounded that he wasn't selected based on the uniqueness of his local hero story. There were over a thousand entrants, all in need of a mobility van so I really wasn't upset that someone else was selected, just shocked that Erik's story wasn't.

The van contest actually struck a weird cord. Competing with other disabled people just didn't seem right. It was somewhat unsettling to think that if my son won, it meant that someone else would lose ~ someone that may need it more. When we learned that Erik didn't win the van, I truly believed that the winning recipient needed it much more than Erik did and that unsettling feeling disappeared instantly.

My Pollyanna personality pointed out the shiny silver lining immediately; at least we wouldn't have to worry about coming up with thousands of dollars to pay the tax liability. My disappointment for Erik was accompanied by happiness for the winners. I imagined their excitement as they received their good news and prayed they would have the resources to pay their tax! After all, even though it was unreliable, Erik already had a van. At least he had something. My heart was heaviest for Mace. He still had nothing.

When we told Erik that he wasn't selected as a winner, all he said was, "I wonder who won?" Then he quickly chirped, "Well I have some work to do! Chuckles, do you want to give me a hand and help me do some repairs on the van?" The two of them spent the entire evening as grease monkeys. Chuck acted as Erik's apprentice and by the end of the evening he proudly donned a mechanic's knuckle, scraped and dirty from participating in blue collar repair work.

As I watched Erik work that night I couldn't have been more proud of him. He was genuinely cheerful as he worked, not spiteful for not having won a new van ~ not pouting, not complaining, just immersing himself in the task at hand ~ doing what he'd always done, making the best of what he had.

At one point he threw himself out of his wheelchair and on to the van floor to work on the track for the sliding side door. We thought he was going to land face-first on the concrete driveway but he recovered valiantly and just kept right on working until he was satisfied he'd done all that he could to extend the life of his old van.

When cleanup started and Chuck went inside to wash his hands and retrieve paper towels, Erik said to me, "Chuck's a good guy. He must really love you, Mom, considering he has to put up with me. I really appreciated his help tonight."

"Yep," I said. "He is a good guy, a really good guy. And we both love you very much. I think he enjoyed learning some mechanic's tricks as much as you appreciated his help."

Erik was right. Not just any man could handle what life had dished out for us. Chuck had been there for us from the get-go, through thick and thin, claiming Erik as one of his own, claiming Jenny as one of his own, claiming their babies as his own grandchildren. Just like Jenny, he never wavered in his love and support for all of us; and our lives were much better, much richer with love, because of him.

17 | surprize

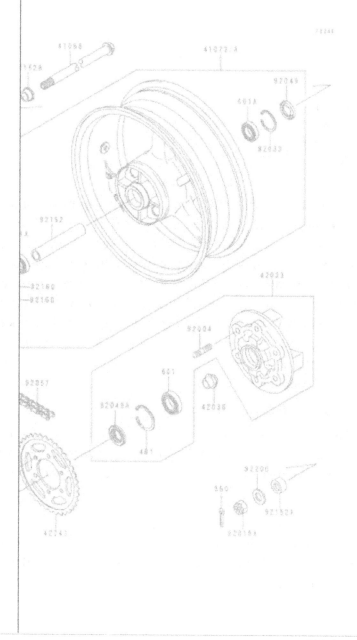

I was so relieved the contest was finally over that for the first time in weeks I slept soundly. I dreamed that I slid down a shiny clean garbage chute along with fluffy stuffing. The bottom of the chute was closed so I was trapped there and the stuffing was falling all around me. Even though the stuffing was as light as a feather, I started to panic, knowing that I'd suffocate if I couldn't find a way out. It was the kind of dream that seemed real. I felt a rush of panic course through my body. Then I suddenly noticed a tiny window inside the chute. I quickly opened it and gasped for air. I could breathe. Thank God, I could breathe. Fresh air never felt so good.

Buzz… Just as I breathed in life-saving fresh air, my phone buzzed and woke me up. Who the heck would be texting me at 7:30 on a Saturday morning? I rested quietly for a few minutes and consciously finished my unsettling dream with deep calm breaths before I picked up the phone to read the text.

It was from Ken and Katie, the folks we visited well over a year ago when their son Zac was recovering from severe brain trauma at New Hanover Regional Medical Center in Wilmington. I wondered what the heck they could be texting about.

Did Erik win the van ?

I responded.

No van, darn...

Thanks for your support.

We think of Zac often especially

since the young man that Erik found

has brain trauma too.

God Bless Us, Everyone.

I didn't know they'd even been following the contest. It was awfully nice of them to check in, but also awfully odd. I hadn't heard from them in over a year. Half an hour later my cell phone rang. Katie was calling me. Why the heck was she texting me and now calling me so early in the morning? I barely answered before she started talking exuberantly. Actually, she was almost screaming.

"Guess what I have for you?

A van for Erik!
free and clear!"

It wasn't just a prize;

it was the ultimate surprize!

My half-opened eyes bugged out of my head. They met with Chuck's half-opened eyes and froze. He thought something dreadful had happened. I could barely speak. I managed a humble "thank you" and muttered a few words of gratitude before I handed the phone to Chuck and fell to my knees beside my bed in tears. Katie's father, who'd used a mobility van, had recently passed. The family decided they wanted Erik to have their father's van; and guess the color ~ dark blue!

The first person I called was my mother. I knew she would think something was wrong because I was still crying. "Mama, everything's okay," I sobbed. Once again I just handed the phone to Chuck. He knew the routine and told the story while I composed myself the best I could.

When he handed the phone back to me, my mother and I cried together and marveled at how God worked in our lives. After I finished crying with my mother, we drove to Erik and Jenny's house to wake them from their Saturday morning sleep and share the news in person. We tried to barge in their house nonchalantly, but my stone-cold shocked face and Chuck's buzzing adrenaline were indications that something was up.

"Family meeting," Chuck announced quietly as he woke everyone. Even though I wasn't crying anymore, I was still shell-shocked and could hardly say a word. So once Chuck had everyone's attention, he just blurted it out. "You have a new van! We just have to go pick it up! It's crazy, I know. But I'm not kidding! You just got your new mobility van!"

With foggy morning eyes, Erik and Jenny sat on the sofa looking at us like we had six heads. "What? Who? What's going on?"

I managed to complete Chuck's announcement with as many details as possible until they finally believed us. "Yes guys. It's real. You have a new van." Their faces reflected mine, stone-cold shock and they were very quiet, very grateful, very humbled.

~

Chuck and I were soon driving to Maryland to retrieve a mobility van for Erik from a complete stranger. Katie's sister, Ann was the caretaker and Power of Attorney for her father's affairs and as we rode with her to have the notary work completed, we each shared a bit of our personal stories with one other. Ann was a strong woman of faith and befittingly named; Ann was also the name of Jesus' grandmother. This woman epitomized the essence of Christ's Grandmother ~ no nonsense with serene kindness.

I began to cry in her car as we drove back from having the documents notarized. "I'm embarrassed and humbled to say that there is a lesson in this for me," I confessed to her. "Until Erik's accident, I never knew how to ask for help. I was always too proud to ask for help and too proud to receive it." Humility, there it was again, showing up when least expected. Ann kept her eyes on the road as I cried, but I could feel her gentle smile as she shared some of her personal story. It was so comforting to listen to her speak; she knew exactly how to graciously acknowledge my confession, like a priest with a repentant parishioner in a private confessional booth, or in this case, a private car ride. A cleansing wash of healing peace came over me with the realization that the most valuable things in life cannot be achieved, only received and only by God's grace.

These people were the real deal. They were God's people, filled with stuff that keeps you believing in the goodness of mankind. Chuck and I just kept looking at each other in disbelief, like we were in some alternate reality. I guess you might call it Heaven. These people, Zac's relatives, literally held the key to a dream we held for Erik ~ the key to a mobility van. We could never have imagined our dream would come true in this way; words of thanks could never convey our gratitude.

~

We arrived at Erik's house with the van on a Thursday evening, physically and emotionally exhausted. Erik wheeled around the van, investigating and assessing what needed to be done in order to make it work for his needs. He has a deep streak of loyalty in him, and I knew what was going through his mind. He was having trouble letting go of the old van. It had seen him through a lot. Both of his miracle children came home from the hospital in that old van, and he knew what he had; even if it was a lot of ongoing maintenance, he knew what he had to do to keep it going. The new van was ~ well… new, to him.

Some people readily accept new things but some tend to become attached to the old stuff. I knew how he felt because I felt the exact same way. And I also knew this van was the most amazing gift that we would ever receive from a stranger. I wasn't quite sure how to reconcile the opposing emotions. Erik remained oddly quiet as he inquisitively meandered about the new van like a dog sniffing out new territory. He finally spoke in a very sincere tone. "I don't want you to think that I'm ungrateful in anyway. I just need to do a few things to make it mine." We respectfully left him alone to complete his sniffing ritual in private.

At 7 o'clock on Saturday morning my phone began to play the tribal music from Erik's ringtone. "Erik Wolfgang?" I answered, still half sleeping.

"Ma, wha'cha doing?" He sounded like the proverbial cat that swallowed the canary.

"Ahhhhh...sleeping. Everything okay?" I wondered what he was up to.

"Yeah, yeah. I've been up all night working on the van. I rebuilt the engine's air intake. I think it's going to work great; more power and better gas mileage. I was wondering if you and Chuck could come over and help me get it all cleaned up?"

I forced my eyelids open, not just from sleepiness but from shock that he had been up all night in his power standing wheelchair, in the garage, working on the engine, making it his own. The last time he pulled an all-nighter, he heard a crash in the middle of the night and ended up saving a young man's life. As I sipped my morning coffee, I shook my head at the irony of the related all-nighters. Chuck and I rousted and made our way over to Erik's garage, bringing the tired mechanic a much needed burger and fries. When we got there, we saw a very tired, very satisfied young man.

June 14, 2014

*Erik after his all night
  mechanical marathon*

As Erik showed us what he had done to refabricate the air intake, we heard a small engine overhead. Chuck and I looked at each other and started laughing. We had a standing joke, maybe more of a standing satire. Every time we heard a small engine in the sky, regardless of our whereabouts, we would say in unison, "There's Ron!" Then Chuck would break into a comedic skit that never failed to make me laugh hysterically, one of those almost-pee-your-pants laughs.

Ron, my ex-husband
is the kind of guy that
could show up anywhere ~
in any kind of contraption!

Does Chitty Chitty Bang Bang
ring a bell?

Over the course of three years, Ron had built his own small airplane, in his garage, from scratch. He had even built the brake to fabricate the metal to build the airplane. He started flying with hang gliders, then moved on to ultralights, then finally graduated to homemade airplanes. It's hard to describe Ron. He's kind of like MacGyver meets Rambo. I've always said that if there was a nuclear disaster, Ron would be the sole survivor, and I'm not exaggerating.

Anyway, I was still laughing hysterically at Chuck's comedic skit as we stepped out of Erik's garage into the driveway to get a look at the plane overhead; and the joke was on us! There he was.

It really was Ron,

in his tiny green homemade airplane,

flying overhead, zooming the house!

Chuck and I never laughed so hard; we could barely catch our breath. It seemed our standing satire was no longer standing. It was flying overhead!

Ron's typical routine was to buzz Erik's house to signal that he needed a ride from the nearby grass field airport, but with an audience of Chuck, myself and the neighbors, Ron couldn't help but put on a show with a few barrel rolls and loops over the treetops. Everyone's jaws fell to the ground; everyone's except Erik's. He just shook his head and grinned.

Since Erik was in the garage all night and morning, he couldn't answer his Magic Jack so he didn't know that his dad was arriving to help him fabricate the driver's seat in the van, but he did know the flyover routine. If a little green plane zooms the house, it's his dad and he needs to be picked up at the airfield a few miles away. That was Saturday at noon. By Saturday night, the driver's seat had been cut and fabricated to fit Erik's long legs, the hand controls had been transferred, the passenger seat had been modified to fit behind the driver's seat and the van had been detailed. My ex-husband and my husband busted their behinds to get it done; and done it was. Now all that remained was to prepare the old van for Mace.

Within the week, Erik and Chuck cleaned the old van and had the oil changed. It was in as good of shape as we could manage and ready for Mace just in time for his benefit at Lyric's Grill and Bar in Burlington. Just a week after Erik had been so graciously gifted with a van he was able to pay it forward. The benefit was a perfect place for Erik and Mace to meet. The Times-News of Burlington covered the story as a follow up to the story they ran regarding the Local Hero Van Contest. Who'd have thought that losing a contest could have such a happy ending?

Erik knew firsthand some of what Mace was going through, and he knew secondhand some of what his caretaker was going through. What impressed me most with my son's behavior that day was when the reporters requested a photo of Mace and Erik with their respective vans, he turned to me and quietly said, "Mom, help her. She needs a break. She's beat."

He was referring to Mace's companion and caretaker, Rhonda. I was taken with his sense of compassion; he immediately picked up on her exhausted state-of-being and his heart went out to her as much as it did to Mace. When the reporter asked what this benefit meant to us, I found myself choking back tears. "We know what it's like to wake up thinking it's just another day and then have your entire life change in an instant."

As I glanced at Erik in his wheelchair my tears stayed lodged in my lower eyelid and I blinked gingerly to keep them from plopping out onto my cheeks. She acknowledged my remark by smiling softly then continued with Erik for a more extensive interview. His words of advice to her readers who may find themselves in this situation were simple.

"You've got to find
your own way.

**The experts may tell you this,
the experts may tell you that.**

But at the end of the day,
**you've got to find
your own way.**"

That day I celebrated life and danced with my granddaughter Mila while Wolfgang stayed snuggled in his carrier. We'd dip and spin as the music played. She'd giggle and reach for my hand as a signal to do it again. Then she pinched me! I welcomed the pinch. It reminded me that she wasn't a dream; none of this was a dream. It wasn't the life I'd planned for myself or for my son. It certainly wasn't the life I'd planned for any of us. But we were all finding our own way on this special journey, in our own special way.

How could we possibly have imagined, that when Chuck and I visited a family two years ago to offer them emotional support after their son was tragically injured, that they would be sharing a gift of this magnitude with our son in his time of need?

June 21, 2014
Erik and Mace at the benefit
in front of their respective vans

Times-News Burlington, NC
Photo courtesy of Scott Muthersbaugh,

18 eyes

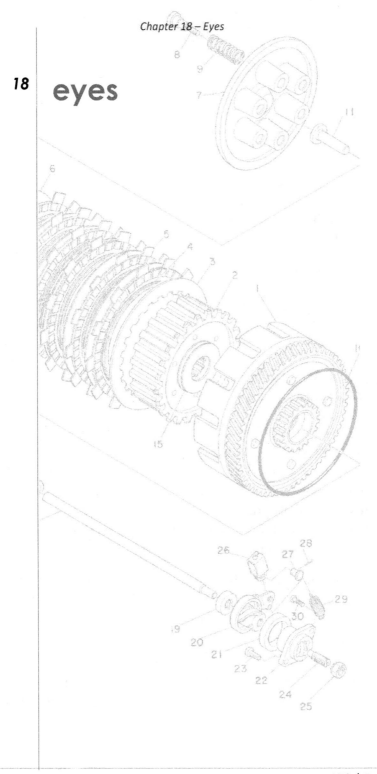

*W*hat a relief it was to have the van ordeal finalized. The day after the benefit, I said to Chuck, "It feels so good to get back to normal." We spent a lazy wonderful Sunday together doing absolutely nothing, respite from the past two months of frenzy. Did I say back to normal? I should know better. There is no more normal, actually there never was, not where Erik is concerned.

Three days after the benefit, I received an email informing me that Erik had been selected as one of the Top Ten Best Dad on Wheels by the Christopher & Dana Reeve Foundation Father's Day campaign to honor outstanding fathers. What? You've got to be kidding me! It was yet another contest that I had almost passed on because I had submitted Erik's story of parenthood via unconventional methods to the Best Dad on Wheels campaign last year and he wasn't selected.

When that same contest rolled around this year it was at the same time we were consumed with the van contest. I was so overwhelmed with campaigning for the van that I passed on the best dad campaign; until I received an email a few days after the van contest ended. That email read, "We have extended the deadline for submissions for the Best Dad on Wheels campaign. Please submit your entrant!" I thought it was kind of odd to extend a deadline so I took it as a sign to ignore the notion that I was a crazy overzealous mom.

I told Chuck that they must not have gotten many entries. Why else would they extend the deadline? Anyway I guess the opportunist in me just couldn't resist. I literally threw together a two hundred word essay along with a photo and hit the submit button. After the disappointment of the van contest my expectation of any response was zero.

My heart just wasn't in it. In truth, a large part of me didn't even want to submit. I'd just die if I had to beg people to vote again! I just couldn't do it. "Not to worry," I reassured myself. "There's no way Erik will be chosen."

I confess. I made the submission with ulterior motives ~ to keep Erik's name circulating in the paralyzed community. The Christopher & Dana Reeve Foundation supports the Frazier Rehabilitation Institute in Louisville, Kentucky which is conducting clinical trials using electrostimulation epidural implants, the same facility that invited Erik to participate in the external stimulation trials a few months ago, of which he graciously declined. He said if he was going to be away from his family for four months with no expenses paid, he wanted more than to participate in the studies of external stimulation. He wanted that epidural implant.

I figured it wouldn't hurt to have his name circulating within the organization. Maybe it would help his chances to someday be selected for the implant. So no harm ~ no foul. It was simply a strategic move by a crazy overzealous mom, but go figure; when you least expect something, it happens. Now I had to tell Erik and Jennifer ~ yikes.

I sheepishly called Jennifer and said, "Okay, please tell me that you won't hate me."

She hesitated, "Oh no, what did you do?"

Again I pleaded, "First, please tell me that you won't hate me?"

Unconvincingly she said, "I don't hate you."

"Okay," I continued. "Now please ask Erik to say he won't hate me."

Erik's unconvincing response was the same. "I won't hate you. Now what did you do?"

I reluctantly delivered the news like a teenager in trouble with their parents. "Erik has been chosen as one of the Top Ten 2014 Best Dad on Wheels by the Christopher & Dana Reeve Foundation."

| *"Not another contest!" Erik growled.* |

"I know! I'm sorry! I never thought you'd get picked, no offense! Not that you're not a great dad. I just wanted to keep your name in circulation because of the Reeves Foundation's affiliation with Frazier Rehab and the epidural implant. I'm so sorry!"

"Ma! You're killing me!" But I could hear a faint smile in his voice.

"Don't worry," I assured him. "We're not campaigning for this one. I'll just post it to Facebook once and notify family because it's such an honor to be acknowledged by the Reeve Foundation."

"Yes, it is really nice," Jenny chimed in. "He's always telling me how I don't appreciate him and how he takes care of our children and that I take him for granted. So now he has printed proof."

Jennifer doesn't get gooey with Erik. If anything she's tough on him; it's exactly what he needs and why he's managed his paralysis so well. Their daily life bantering sounds just like the stereotypical work-at-home mom and the conventional-job dad, except the traditional roles are reversed. So we printed the internet page that listed him as one of the Top Ten 2014 Best Dad on Wheels, framed it and placed it next to his helmet in the curio. That way, he can feel appreciated every time he sees it.

A few months later, Erik was selected to receive the Stephen E. Sallee Award of Excellence for Assistive Technology User at the 2014 NCATP Conference. When the award presenter summarized Erik's story and called him to receive his award, a standing ovation broke out.

October 23, 2014   *Photo courtesy of NCATP*

Erik with the NC Assistance Technology Program presenters, holding the Stephen E. Sallee Award of Excellence for Assistive Technology User

Erik was so filled with emotion that he was rendered speechless. The crowded room waited patiently for him to compose himself until the words from his heart found his voice.

"Thank you, very much. I had prepared a speech actually, for accepting this, but I normally shoot better from the hip and I've been told I'm brutally honest, so bear with me if I start out a little rocky. It'll be worth it in the end."

There was a long pause as emotion spilled from his eyes again. "It's gonna be tough, but here we go." Erik's voice cracked, but he managed to speak in bits and pieces as he cried through this entire acceptance message:

~

"I look around here today and I see some incredibly heroic people. What you do on a daily basis, I'm sure sometimes seems mundane - paperwork, filing everything, out there visiting people. But what you do is give people back the ability to live a full life. So yes, this award is presented to me, but it's yours. You're a testament to mankind. It's a big deal. I didn't think it was going to be this hard to say it. Please everybody here, stand and give yourself a round of applause. You're the ones who made this possible."

~

As he spoke, his audience cried right along with him. There wasn't a dry eye in the house. Erik's genuine humility pierced each and every soul. Later that afternoon, Erik addressed a group of convention attendees as a guest speaker and shared his personal story. During Q&A he was asked, "What advice can you give us as professionals on how to help encourage patients through the rehab process?"

He answered the inquiry without hesitation.

~

"That's a good question and I have a good answer for you. When I was going through my rehab - and I know this is going to sound sappy but I've cried in front of you guys already so I don't care - what made the biggest impact in my rehab was my ability to interact with my family. When you're going through rehab, it's not about the equipment. It's not about your broken bones. It's about your need to survive and what that is. If you don't have a reason to survive, you're going to pull the trigger. Even someone with no injuries at all can have such a diminished capacity of mind that they want to take their own life and not fight for it. So that's where rehab starts; it starts with a reason to live. Once you have a reason to live, or at least some motivation to live, you try to succeed and overcome the obstacles, whatever they are. So, that's the key. If you can find out what motivates them, I guarantee your results will be impressive. You can give people all the shiny fancy toys in the world but unless they want to succeed for the right reasons, none of that will matter.
It all hinges on a reason to live - on purpose."

~

Right off the cuff, Erik answered the question that was posed with an eloquently delivered message that summarized how he'd made it from the place of tragedy and despair to the place of fairytales by discovering new purpose and a reason to live.

And his reasons to live continue. Erik and Jennifer moved back to Wilmington in 2016 and lived with Jennifer's mother while they worked tirelessly for four years with the invaluable help of Erik's father along with other family, friends, and even strangers, to literally build their own home in Hampstead, North Carolina.

They also dusted off the bull machine to make another baby boy, and I witnessed the birth our third precious grandchild!

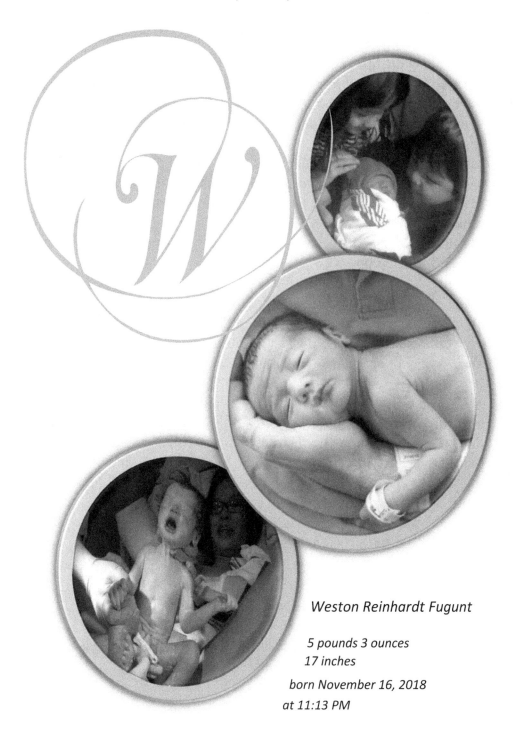

Weston Reinhardt Fugunt

5 pounds 3 ounces
17 inches
born November 16, 2018
at 11:13 PM

Once in a while life grants us a fairytale. Not that anyone wishes to be paralyzed in a motorcycle accident at age twenty-five, but tragedy is what sets the stage for triumph and warrants the making of a fairytale ~ in this case, a real life fairytale.

Make no mistake; real life fairytales lives are not perfect nor are they easy. Fairytales lives are created, choice by choice, day by grueling day; moments in time that are to be treasured and honored as extraordinary; something that Erik and Jennifer exemplify on their quest to rebuild a life and create a family of their own. As Erik would put it, "Sometimes fairytales are just stories of perseverance."

If you would have asked me, at the time of Erik's accident, how I thought his life would look five years later, I would never, in my wildest dreams, have been able to imagine such an unbelievable, continuing saga that is the everyday ordinary life of my son and his family.

And if you were to ask me what will happen in the next five years or the next fifty-five years, I'd have to answer the same way that I answered Erik when we sat on a park bench together when I visited him on his birthday so many years ago. "I don't know. I don't know if we're supposed to know." What I do know is that my son embodies his Fourth of July birthright; he lives life with independence and fireworks.

~

Every so often, I think back to Erik's prophetic 21st birthday,
and what he said to me...

"Mom, I feel like I was sent here for a purpose ~
like I was born
to do something important
that could change
the course of the world.

And it feels like
it might be tragic.

Do you think you know
when it happens,
when you've done that
which you're sent her to do?"

All Erik has to do is look into the eyes of his own children to answer that question. I believe his life is right on purpose. That blessed Goodwill stranger said it best when he looked into Erik's eyes so many years ago. Perhaps one day this book will find its way into that stranger's hands; or perhaps that godly stranger's hands and his gift of the Saint Benedict Crucifix made the way for this book as he wished us Godspeed.

"I haven't seen eyes that deep for a long time.

Your son has the eyes of Jesus."

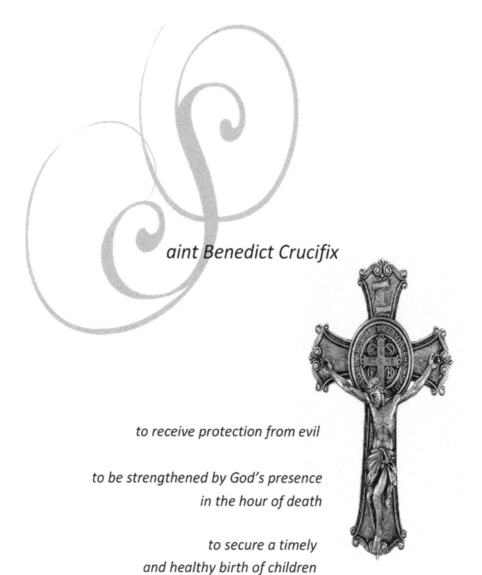

aint Benedict Crucifix

to receive protection from evil

*to be strengthened by God's presence
in the hour of death*

*to secure a timely
and healthy birth of children*

Afterword

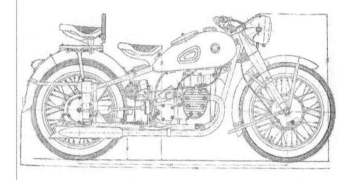

AFTERWORD

by Erik Fugunt

Before My Accident

I had much
more than a
typical youth.
I was very active
and outgoing and had a
tendency to take risks ~ a lot of
risks. For some reason I always
felt the need to take those risks
and push my limits, just for me ~
not to impress anyone ~ because
most of the time no one was
around anyway. I just pushed the
limits for myself.

I started out really young riding motorcycles and horses. We lived in a
rural area so those things were available, fun to do and an easy outlet for
constructive behaviors, at least better than the alternatives. So, that's how
I grew up, racing motorcycles, 4-H horseshows, swimming, boating ~
any kind of outdoor activity. I raced motocross until I was twelve years
old. Then I moved, along with my father from Pennsylvania to
Wilmington, North Carolina.

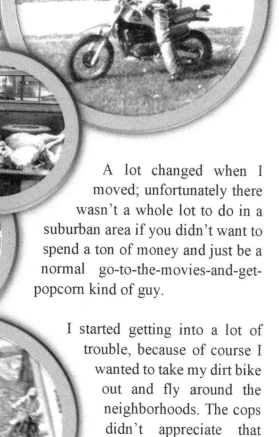

A lot changed when I moved; unfortunately there wasn't a whole lot to do in a suburban area if you didn't want to spend a ton of money and just be a normal go-to-the-movies-and-get-popcorn kind of guy.

I started getting into a lot of trouble, because of course I wanted to take my dirt bike out and fly around the neighborhoods. The cops didn't appreciate that very much and that caused a whole slew of other problems.

So I got a street bike and started doing professional stunt riding. It came pretty natural to me because I took what I learned from motocross racing and converted it over to stunt riding. But you don't make any money doing it. Even though you might be stunting professionally, you don't really make any money because you blow an engine or pop a tire at a show and there goes your profit. And you do that every show. So you're just paying for your habit. You do it because it's fun to watch people light up.

When I was nineteen I moved to Daytona Beach, Florida to attend motorcycle technician school and do what I loved, stunt ride and work on bikes. I graduated from the American Motorcycle Institute and moved to Maryland where I continued to pursue that career and lifestyle. It was a great time. I met a lot of great people and rode with some great stunt riders.

Throughout that progression, I would transfer to stunt teams wherever I went because most of them are small and locally based. From Wilmington to Daytona Beach to Maryland, it's all the same. No matter where you go, you just fit into that crazy clique. Stunt teams adopt riders quickly ~ the ones that can do it, anyway. People will hire you to perform anywhere they think they can draw a crowd. From Daytona Bike Week, to fairs, to rallies, wherever. They pay you a couple hundred bucks ~ pays for your tires! Risk was everyday life for me and no big deal.

I guess the reason behind taking all these risks started out as overcoming fears. It started out as fear to jump a ditch then you become a great motocross rider. And then it goes into fear of drowning and you become a great swimmer.

You just have a fear and then try to overcome it, even if it's fear of death. You push it. You find out where that fine line is and then you try to ride that line. Some of it is adrenaline, some of it is challenging the unknown, and some of it is a sense of adventure.

There's an element to
**having your
life in danger**

that **sharpens your senses.**

It's hard to explain. Some people call it "being in the zone". You know, when you see an NBA player shooting a basketball and he's in the zone, he gets swish after swish. Take that and multiply it by ten when you're on a motorcycle because if you fail, you die. So when you're in the zone, you're really in the zone.

After a few years in Maryland, I moved back to North Carolina, back to Wilmington. I started growing older and kind of coming out of it, but you can't breed out riding. You can't quit it. It's like the drug that never ends. Anyway, I went back to school at Cape Fear Community College for Marine Technology to study underwater surveying, mapping, sonar, instrumentation, things like that. The idea was to eventually go searching for oil and burn the planet! There's money in it; how about it? Who would have thought?

Everything was great. I was doing well in school, getting straight A's, riding bikes, stunting, flying airplanes, boating, and lovin' the water at the beach ~ overall enjoying myself.

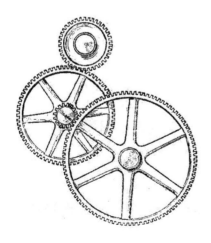

My Accident

I was in a new relationship with a young lady and we were actually about to fly down to Florida for a fly-in, which is like a festival for pilots and aircraft; and I was really excited about getting home to meet Jenny and get on our way. I just got out of my morning classes at school. It was a great day. The pavement was real warm; tires were sticky. I headed for home on a road that I traveled so many times, it had become second nature. It had a lot of turns that were more like track turns than actual street turns.

One turn in particular had a real sharp high camber; it was the last turn before I reached home, of course. Normally, you could come into it and get your knee down. There aren't too many turns on the street you can do that on. Anybody that rides knows that. You've got to have the right turn. This particular one was it. You could come into it pretty hot and slide the rear out. When you start to slide it out, you accelerate and the tire will hook up, the bike will lift up, do a yaw ~ a wheel stand out of the turn ~ and roll up into straight position. Then shew, you're gone. Moto GP racers do it all the time, on every turn, but that's because every turn on the Moto GP track is perfect. They're made for it. There was only one turn on this road that could handle it, so I always liked to come in and hit that turn hard.

On that particular day as I came into the turn hot, about half way through it, I noticed debris. It looked like a trail of slime that went from the top of the turn all the way down to the apex and there was just no avoiding it. Obviously I recognized that it was probably going to be a problem. So you just hold on. You're committed at that point anyway. The best you can do is to keep your line and hope that the tires hold. But unfortunately they didn't.

So I low-sided the bike and it ricocheted off the curb and went flying. But because the human body doesn't quite ricochet like a bike, I tumbled end over end and slid about fifty yards into a planter before I made impact with a big oak tree. I know I came in at excessive speed. I was moving, probably 75 to 80 mph. It was a hard hit.

When you ride and take risks, you don't take unnecessary risks. I always wore full gear, a full leather jacket and a really good high dollar racing helmet. You protect yourself as much as you can. You don't want to be stupid and honestly if it wouldn't have been for that tree, I probably would have walked away from the accident. But I caught that oak tree and that was the end of it. Even the best gear doesn't protect against impact with an oak tree. So that's what paralyzed me.

I broke all the ribs on my left side, my pelvis, hand and scapula. My high dollar racing helmet had a nice split down the back of it. But the life threatening part of the accident came from the way my ribs shattered and acted like claws that lacerated my lung. And of course once my lung was shredded, the whole air sac cavity began to fill with blood. And that was it. I sort of remember lying there, just a little bit. I remember feeling very peaceful. I knew I was pretty torn up because I vaguely remember trying to move and I couldn't. I remember gasping for air but it was real foggy. I was in and out of it.

I don't remember the ambulance ride or the people that were there helping me. So the entire incident and my arrival at the ER Trauma Unit at New Hanover Regional Medical Center were unknown to me for the most part. I found out later that when I arrived to the ER, I had already flat lined twice in the ambulance, then a third time on the ER table. They weren't getting vitals. They weren't able to get oxygen to my lungs and it was to the point where they debated whether it was worth continuing to try and save me. I'd flat lined so many times and oxygen was so low that they really weren't sure if I had good brain function.

So it came down to a vote. Half of the emergency room team voted yes and the other half of the emergency room team voted no. The half that voted yes kept trying. They split my left side open through the shattered ribs with a rough cut from the middle of my chest to the back of my armpit. My left lung fell out in pieces and a pool of blood. They soon figured out they were intubating the wrong lung. The respiratory specialist told me, "It was just intuition. Man, I just knew it. I knew that right lung was good. I just had to get a tube in there." He finally got an oxygen line into my right lung, which was still intact.

Then they raced me down the hallway with their hands still in my chest to clamp the aorta and save any remaining blood to my brain, burst into an empty operating room, stitched my left lung back together, buttoned me up and waited.

So my life came down to a coin toss,
a fifty-fifty coin toss,

and the toss favored me.

I have no hard feelings against the side that voted no. I'm not one hundred percent sure what I would have done if I were in their position. I don't know if I would have called it or not. You can't put yourself into that position if you're not actually there. Not only is it a moral call, it's a technical one as well. You just don't know what you'd do until you're in that position.

I had no idea that any of this had happened. I was put into an induced coma and placed on an infant respirator with hopes that my left lung would heal and hold oxygen. And at that point, no one really expected me to live.

The next thing

I remember was waking up in the hospital.

I had no idea what was going on. I was looking around like, "I'm in the hospital. Something must've happened."

There was a doctor standing there and he said, "You were in a really, really severe accident."

I was thinking, "Oh God, okay, great. So here we go again." But I noticed that I couldn't move my arm so I was thinking, "Argh, I broke my arm. I broke my arm." And I'm trying to do a body assessment real quick. "Okay, arms work ~ and check. Neck's good. Alright, that's important ~ check." And I noticed that I couldn't speak. And I thought, "Something's up. Why can't I talk correctly?" I came to realize that I had a breathing tube down my throat to assist my lacerated left lung.

Of course, when you're just waking up and starting to figure everything out, you don't realize what's going on. But slowly it starts to unfold. You have tubes hanging all over you. I first thought that I was just in a little accident, but it soon became a stark realization.

Holy Shit.

I was in a real accident

~ a really bad accident.

After ten or fifteen minutes of trying to communicate I found out that I was paralyzed. The doctor just said, "You sustained a spinal cord injury that crushed your T8 and T9 vertebrae. You won't walk again."

I didn't believe him. I'm thinking, "You're lying. Whatever Doc. Forget you. I'm getting out of here. Hurry up. I got things to do." I had no idea that it was even a week later and that I had missed my fly-in... Once I found that out, I was really upset ~ like I didn't have other things to be upset about. I teetered in ICU for eighteen days before I was stable enough to undergo a five hour spinal fusion. I have twelve inch titanium rods down either side of my spine to hold it in place since two of the vertebrae were completely shattered. That surgery was brutal. The postop was extremely painful. The Dilaudid drip for pain was an absolute necessity and even then it didn't take care of the pain.

My Rehabilitation

I was moved to the adjacent rehab hospital four days after that spinal fusion surgery, so I healed rather quickly considering the severity of my condition. That surgery was so excruciating and painful because they actually bolt the rods into your vertebrae at two or three places below the injury, bridge that injury with the rods, and then put two or three screws above the injury. I could feel those screws drilled in to my vertebrae above the injury.

After the spinal fusion, I was able to sit up without folding like an accordion. Then comes rehab where they teach you very basic functions ~ how to feed yourself, how to dress yourself, and how to move around in a wheelchair ~ because obviously they know you're going to be chair bound. I had a shattered shoulder so I couldn't move my arm for a month. But once my arm started to heal and I was able to move it again, I learned how to transfer out of a wheelchair into another seat.

Some of those rehabilitation lessons were things that you didn't expect, like how to urinate, which would be all catheterization now because I had no muscle control over my bladder. That's a pain in the ass, but pretty straight forward. Putting a cath in and out, anybody knows it's not rocket science.

Rehab was mostly learn-as-you-go. You fall out of the chair and you miss a transfer and you bust your face, but you pick yourself back up and keep on going. That's just another obstacle to jump over. The one thing that irritated me most was the bowel control issues. Since you have a no control over your bowel muscles, your bowel evacuates whenever it's ready to. That's not only difficult to plan around, it's immobilizing and dehumanizing.

Defecating on yourself all the time is not exactly something you want to think about. And although everybody's going to get there sooner or later, you don't want to get there at age twenty-five. It's a very difficult and private thing to overcome. Most people don't even feel comfortable using the restroom facilities in front of other people much less having somebody else do it for you. I'm pretty outgoing so I didn't have a problem with that. If a nurse needed to take care of me and do my bowel program in bed, whatever, that was fine; but you still want to have a sense of independence over that.

You don't want to have to rely on somebody else. For me it was completely unacceptable. So coming up with inventive ways of dealing with that burden was one of my top priorities in rehab, whether it was for them or not. Everything's a little backwards at a hospital with a lot of bureaucracy involved. They'll come in and wake you up to make sure that you're sleeping. Once they check that you're sleeping they'll say, "Okay. You're on schedule to sleep so you can go back to sleep now."

So, when you're in the rehab, they teach and recommend that you try a couple of different bowel routines. Everybody's a little different so everybody has a different way of doing things and they'll tell you that straight off. What they suggest is to use a suppository, because everything at the hospital is on a schedule.

They'll come at 3:35 on the dot and they'll roll you over on your side and they'll take a small little egg shaped capsule and insert it into your rectum. Then they'll come back thirty minutes later and roll you onto a bed pan and say, "Okay it's time." Normally they get it somewhat close. And they'll just leave you on there until you evacuate and you've had your bowel movement for that day. That's all great when you're in the hospital but when you transition from a rehab hospital where you have round the clock care to an environment where you're trying to take care of yourself, life doesn't operate on schedules.

So they give you other options for your bowel program, one of which is manual extraction. And that's pretty much exactly what it sounds like. You use your fingers to manually extract stool from your colon. Then there's good old digital stimulation which is like manual extraction but you don't have to dig. You just use your finger to trick your body by placing it in your rectum or at the opening of the anus and the body responds with a reflex muscle action to evacuate your bowel. Even though you don't have feeling you can still have reflexive muscle memory. It says, "Okay. I don't need a brain to tell me this. I already know it on my own." It's a reflex response. It usually worked for me and it wasn't as bad as digging but it still took time.

Once I was able to be lifted out of bed, the rehab staff had me on a routine of inserting my suppository and then shuttling me onto a commode and letting me sit there for an hour or however long it took. And yeah, some of the stool would come out. Then they would say, "Okay. It's time to get in the shower." I'd be sitting in the shower and some more of my stool would come out. I was like, "Something's wrong. This doesn't make sense." I was frustrated and if nothing else, I knew this much about my hospital bowel program:

There's got to be a better way ~
a more accurate and precise way
to do this.

So early in my rehab I began experimenting, with water, the method of common sense. Anyone who's ever had diarrhea knows that when there's water in your colon there's just no holding it back. So I used the detachable shower head as a way to get water into my colon and began doing that every day during rehab. They'd take me to the toilet and give me a suppository. I would sit there for about five minutes and say, "Okay! I'm getting in the shower!" Without them watching, I would perform my bowel program in the shower, then my mother would clean up the stool on the shower floor and flush it down the toilet. No one else knew what was going on and we kept it that way.

I knew my shower method was working in conjunction with the suppository but I wanted to bypass the suppository altogether to help avoid having accidental discharges. Unfortunately, you have to jump through hoops when you're in a rehab hospital to make everybody happy. So I waited until I arrived home to try my water induced bowel program without the suppository. I immediately built a device that mimicked my shower routine, but right over the toilet. It was easy and surprisingly it worked extremely well, even without the suppository. It reduced my bowel program time from at least forty-five minutes to less than ten minutes. And better yet, I didn't have to clean up bowel movements from my girlfriend's shower…which leads me to Jennifer.

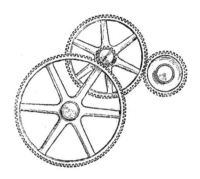

My Relationship with Jennifer

I knew Jennifer for a very brief time during high school, then I moved away. But eight years later, when I moved back to Wilmington, thankfully we reconnected; it was about two months before the accident. She found me on Facebook. It was crazy how we seemed to be at the same stage in our lives where we both wanted a serious relationship and a family. We committed to each other very quickly and I couldn't imagine any better life partner.

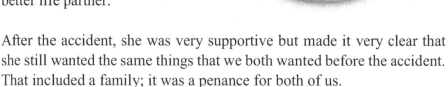

After the accident, she was very supportive but made it very clear that she still wanted the same things that we both wanted before the accident. That included a family; it was a penance for both of us.

During my recovery, we were still somewhat dating. I was still courting her to the best of my abilities. Considering I was pretty banged up and in the hospital, it was hard but we still managed to have a lot of fun. Even though it was an extremely difficult time, we made the best of it. When she asked me to move to her house as soon as I was released from rehab, we had a serious heart-to-heart sit down about what could be expected of life from here on out, and whether or not we were both still game. Surprisingly, she was still game to put up with it ~ to deal with what life had thrown at us. It came down to this:

We both still loved each other
very much and we both
still wanted the same things.

The deciding factor
would be our ability
to have a family
in light of my injuries.

And although we didn't
know what it would
entail,

we were both determined
to make it happen
and decided
to make a go of it.

There wasn't a lot of information available about being able to conceive as a paraplegic. Most of the information and resources we found were more of a generic treatment for mainstream male infertility ~ for a male that has less than average sperm count or an inability to inseminate a female due to low quality sperm.

But paraplegic male fertility obstacles and male infertility are completely different. A paraplegic that has completely normal sperm count and reproduction capabilities before the injury can still have the exact same capabilities after the injury. Nothing changes except some paraplegics can't feel sensation or have an ejaculation.

So for a man, the inability to conceive due to paralysis can be completely different than the inability to conceive due to quality sperm issues. Currently, some of the medical field's fertility experts and specialists view them as the same but there are other avenues that can be explored for paraplegic men.

I think it comes down to money ~ to monetary motivation on the behalf of some doctors; because in my case, the avenue that was most effective to retrieve healthy sperm, electroejaculation, wasn't that expensive. But the local fertility specialist we chose completely dismissed the option of electroejaculation, stating it wasn't very effective, and he strongly recommended traditional in vitro. So we agreed to use a credit card and try it.

Since we had a special twist to our case, no sperm sample, it added a small complication on top of regular in vitro. They had to retrieve a sperm sample via a testicular biopsy, which means they surgically entered the scrotum and took a small portion of my testicle to extract immature sperm. The sperm contained in that biopsy weren't exactly fully matured. So even though they had all the DNA makeup of fully matured sperm, they were still small and weak, premature.

Once those sperm were collected, they were allowed to mature a few days before they inseminated the eggs. That was the recommended method of sperm retrieval that the local fertility specialist made for me as a paraplegic male. So even though I knew other methods existed, I followed along and decided to go through with it.

Meanwhile, Jenny had taken medication that stimulated egg production because the more eggs they have to inseminate, the better the chances that one of them will take. Out of the six eggs that she produced, four of them were high quality eggs and able to be fertilized. Out of the four that were fertilized with my almost-mature sperm, two of them took and were actually incubated. From the two that were incubated and implanted, we don't know how many actually impregnated, but we believe at least one of them did because we had a positive pregnancy blood test. Unfortunately it wasn't a full fertilization. She stopped testing positive after two weeks.

In vitro is expensive and we knew we wanted more than one child. For us to continue with in vitro would have cost upwards of thirty or forty thousand dollars if not more; sky's the limit depending on if it took or not. They say they have high success rates but it's a roll of the dice just like anything else. And using immature sperm doesn't help roll the dice in our favor. We had used a credit card to finance the first attempt. If we kept that up, we'd be financially sunk. That summer was emotionally tough. We were trying everything we could at home to get a healthy sperm sample naturally but nothing was working.

Making Babies

We kept our wits through that summer but almost went crazy trying to get our own sample at home. Then ironically, I was contacted by The Miami Project to Cure Paralysis, a research hospital located in Miami Beach, Florida. They specialize in spinal cord research and try to solve the issues that paralyzed people encounter every day. We had applied for their male fertility program about a year before, but unfortunately there had been an overlap between clerics and our application was somehow overlooked during the transition.

When they contacted me, I learned more about the method called electroejaculation, a somewhat hand-me-down technology from animal husbandry. Farmers and herders have been using this technique for years and years to artificially inseminate their herds with great success. The Miami Project was using this same technology in their facility for human trials with paralyzed men.

I was nervous when I scheduled the appointment to have the initial testing and research done. But I'd gone through a testicular biopsy with no anesthesia, so I'm thinking to myself, "If I can watch somebody operate on my scrotum then there's probably a pretty good chance that whatever they can dish out, I can take!"

And it was fine. The procedure was extremely comfortable and easy to do. As a matter of fact, I decided I could probably do it on my own ~ even though the doctors warned me that the procedure should only be performed by medical professionals.

We did the best we could to schedule the electroejaculation procedure at The Miami Project so that it would coincide with Jenny's ovulation time. I was confident that I could inseminate her by myself at the facility in Miami as soon as they retrieved my sperm sample ~ if the procedure worked. And it did. The electroejaculation procedure was a success. I was able to produce a full sample, the same as I had before the accident. I inseminated Jenny almost immediately. Unfortunately the timing of her ovulation wasn't just perfect. So there was no conception that time. But I'd seen the device. I'd seen the procedure. I'd seen it work successfully. I understood the mechanics behind it and knew how it was done. I was fairly convinced that if I could get my own electrostimulation machine, not only could I do it myself, I'd also be able to use it whenever I needed.

So once again, there's that element of convenience for someone who's paralyzed ~ the convenience of getting sperm samples when you need them not, "Okay, we can get a sample once in a blue moon, but is it on the ovulation day?" With this technique, not only could I get the sample on her ovulation day but I could do it more than once on ovulation day. It was brilliant. So my search for an electrostimulation machine began.

The first machine that I was able to acquire was a handheld battery operated device used on goats and sheep. It peaked at three and one half volts. The samples that I obtained from using that machine were decent but they weren't the same volume that was retrieved with the machine in Miami.

Even so, we used the smaller sperm sample to inseminate and we did achieve a pregnancy. That pregnancy lasted a little over six weeks but didn't produce a heartbeat. But at least we achieved conception on our first at-home attempt. I knew from the trials at The Miami Project that I required five to six volts or more. So in my case, the goat machine just didn't have enough juice behind it to produce a quality sample.

The only machine that I knew would produce a full sample for me was a bovine electrostimulation ejaculator ~ the bull machine. So I searched relentlessly until I found one and bought it. I did need to make one slight modification. Since the rectal probe from the goat machine was the correct size for me, I re-wired that probe to my newly acquired bull machine. Once that modification was complete I was ready for some trial runs. It took quite a leap of faith on my part but luckily I had the assurance of a mechanical background and made sure that I did all my voltage and ohm checks to ensure that everything was working properly.

Next, I prepared a clean area, something without any contaminants around, like hair or dust ~ stuff like that. I used my bed and put a clean sheet down, just like they would do in a hospital. I made sure everything was clean. I specifically made sure my equipment was clean and tested to avoid malfunctions. From there it was a pretty straight forward process. Believe it or not, even the animal husbandry probes come with instructions on how to use them. Who would've thought?

The first two or three tests produced great samples. I wanted to make sure that I had good sperm samples so I set up a lab at the house and did test platelets to check for sperm motility and count. It was amazing to see because I had been testing my own semen seepage for so long with no results. And I'll tell ya what, going through all that and then actually getting a sample and watching all my little soldiers swim around;

| *I was ecstatic! I was yelling through the house, "I got 'em! I got 'em!"* |

And I'm not a doctor but from what I could tell everything looked fine. So we decided to continue with the process.

Obviously, the machines that they are using at Miami are not the same machines that they are using for animal husbandry. They don't have the same safety regulations on animal machines that they would need to have on human machines.

One of the differences would be an addition of a temperature sensing probe on the human machine so that if there was a thermal heat problem with the probe, it would immediately shut down. I didn't have that luxury so I had to be very careful.

I tested it to make sure no dangerous heat was involved and worked slowly and gradually until I achieved ejaculation. I already knew what voltage I responded to because I had gone through the procedure at the Miami Project.

You don't just jump in and hit yourself

with twenty-four volts!

That's enough to bring an elephant down!

Using that procedure, I was able to leave it on for about five seconds at six volts for probably four or five contractions and I was able to get a full sample.

Some people asked if we were afraid of an infection in the uterus. And even though there is a very small chance that could happen we were willing to take that risk. You can get an infection from a cut. You can get infections anywhere, even if you go to the doctor and to what is considered a sterile environment. You have MRSA running rampant in the hospitals. Risk of infection is everywhere. We were clean and careful, so there was really no reason for us not to take a calculated risk. We discussed the possibility of sterility from a uterine infection and, well, I'll just say it. We didn't care. Having a child together was worth the risk.

I hate to say it,
but most of the time
I feel more comfortable
with my life in my own hands
than I do with it
in somebody else's hands.

I don't care how many
books you read,
when it comes down to it,

you're responsible for your own life.

When Jenny saw the sample from the bull machine ejaculation, she was anxious. She knew it was a quality sample. We inseminated. She was still very nervous. After we took the first pregnancy test and it came out positive, she was ecstatic - completely ecstatic. There's no explanation that I could give that would do it justice. When a woman finds out that after two years of trying to achieve a pregnancy she's finally had success, it's amazing. She went from being terrified and not knowing if she would have children to being completely ecstatic; dancing around the house; keeping pregnancy strips; putting them in little picture frames. Any woman who's had problems trying to conceive knows that a positive pregnancy test is something to celebrate. The fact that this was our very first attempt using a great sperm sample from the bull machine was even more reassuring.

The pregnancy developed a good heartbeat and went full term. It was the first recorded case that The Miami Project had of an at-home pregnancy using this technique, ever. As far as we could tell and as far as our doctors could tell, it was a completely normal pregnancy besides that fact that we used the at-home electrostimulation ejaculation and insemination process without approval from The Miami Project.

Ultimately our visit to The Miami Project was priceless. Not only was it a privilege to participate in their research, it provided me with the firsthand experience that gave me the confidence to do it myself. I was actually able to observe exactly how the procedure was done ~ on me. And I learned what voltage initiated my ejaculation. I knew from their tests that my sperm sample was high quality. If it weren't for The Miami Project, I wouldn't have a family now. My experience there enabled me to pursue the process at home by myself.

So yeah, it was quite a leap and not just with the technology, because the technology already existed. It took a leap of faith on our part to take the hits and blows and miscarriages; and to have the gumption to go through with it and decide that having a family was worth taking the risks ~

~ the risk of injuring myself, the risk of infection, the risk of potential miscarriage, the risk of failure. But these risks happen every single day and for no apparent reason.

For me personally, it meant that

I was not a failure.
I was able to have a family.

There are so many people in my exact position that are searching for answers, trying to find a way to have a normal stable life. And to be able to give this hope to somebody in that position is just incredible. It's like Neil Armstrong walking on the moon. Like, "Here humanity, have this!" It's pretty awesome to just give it away, not only for me but for the Miami Project as well, to do these clinical trials and give that information to me without a fee 'cause it's not like I just came up with it on my own.

Yes, I tested it on my own and tried it on my own and made it work on my own, but for them to share their knowledge with me was incredible and it was the major contributing factor to my success. It's everybody working together for the greater good. I really feel privileged to be part of it and I am deeply grateful to have my three beautiful children because of it.

Mila, Wolfgang, and Weston
Spring 2019

Becoming a Parent

My own personal belief is that we are here to pass down our knowledge and wisdom and experiences to the next generation. That's our purpose ~ to push forward, to discover the unknown and to teach the little bit that we've learned to our own children.

So for me,

becoming a parent means that

**I got to play a part
in the great order.**

That's tremendous.

I want my children to have a loving, open, productive childhood and life. It's hard to describe. Parenting is a dichotomy. You want to expose your children to everything and teach them everything you can, but on the other hand you're trying to protect them from everything as well.

During my childhood, I was exposed to a great deal and it led me to where I am today ~ the failures and successes that I've had. So I know that I teach them now is going to serve them rest of their lives.

You just hope and pray that
they're able to find
their own way,

and do what makes
them happy.
No regrets.

When you're growing up you always hear, "You just wait until you have a little boy or a little girl. You wait until you have your kid. It changes you." And it does. It certainly does. I know that I'm in for some torture. I'm sure of it. You definitely have an appreciation for what your parents have gone through, and what parents have gone through for generations and generations, and what parents are going to go through in future generations.

Living Courageously

People often ask if I would change what I did in my past. I wouldn't change anything ~ absolutely not. As a matter of fact, if I could do it all over again, I would for sure. There's no replacement. I've lived more in the first twenty some years of my life than most people will live in a lifetime or two or three. I can honestly say that. And I'm still pushing the limits. What served me well in the past is still serving me well now.

Jennifer doesn't approve of my risk-taking all the time. She comes from a more conservative side of the spectrum so her idea of risk-taking isn't exactly the same as mine. And although she supports my crazy habits sometimes, I have definitely been restrained a little bit by her. The risks I take now are much more calculated. But she understands that being a risk-taker and being aggressive is a way to get things done. And when you push your limits you learn new things about yourself. That's one of the byproducts. If Mila and Wolfgang and Weston turn out to be risk-takers, I'd be ecstatic. There's nothing that would make me happier because that's living. And I'll make sure they wear helmets.

It's important to look at obstacles as an opportunity to get your ass in gear because the transition to becoming a more adventurous person after an injury can be extremely difficult. In my case, I just say, "I'm already paralyzed. What's the worst that could happen?"

Since the injury, I run into problems all the time, stupid little things that you would never normally think about, like getting down stairs. Before, the big problem was, "Can I jump the ditch?" or "How big of a wave can I catch out on the surf?" But now it's, "Well, I'm pretty sure I can get down those five to six stairs without killing myself in this chair." And you just do it.

Youthful risk-taking certainly affected my life

in positive and negative ways, obviously.

I'm paralyzed now because of it.

But at the same time, it's that same mentality from

youthful risk-taking that led me to more careful and calculated risk-taking,

and that has given me my family.

Don't get me wrong. My process wasn't instant. You have to make a decision early on. You can either stop, because obviously if you're more of a risk-taker, you're not real terrified of death anyway. So you take that into consideration and ask yourself, "Well does it end here or do I roll the dice and see what I can make of it?"

You have to make that decision before you can move out of depression ~ that state of, "Oh my God, why did this happen to me; why didn't they just leave me on the side of the road?" Before you can move out of that, you have to make up your mind whether or not you're going to try. Once you decide to try, it's all downhill and you can really start making progress.

Out of everything that I went through, the accident; the miscarriages; the trials and suffering; the whole nine yards; if I had one thing that I could share with others, it would be without a doubt to follow their instincts. Take that leap of faith, look into the unknown and try to find what you're looking for, because without risk there's really no hope. To sum it up,

If there's one thing I've learned

from my experiences, my successes and failures alike,

it would be to live courageously.

...and they lived

courageously

ever after

cour . age { noun }

Strength in the face
of pain or grief;

Quality of mind or spirit
that enables a person
to face difficulty, danger, and pain,

without fear...

The End

September 2019

Erik and family with his father, Ron

Erik and family with his mother, Jacque and other father, Chuck

December 2018

*Erik and family with
Jennifer's mother, Ivy*

*In Honorable
& Loving Memory
of Jennifer's father,
Siu Lun Wu
1943 – 2016*

IN CELEBRATION

OF ETERNAL LIFE

Erik's ICU Nurse and our dear friend

Louise "Weezie" Lanter

1960-2015

"*Legends say that hummingbirds float free of time, carrying our hopes for love, joy and celebration. Hummingbirds open our eyes to the wonder of the world and inspire us to open our hearts to loved ones and friends. Like a hummingbird, we aspire to hover and to savor each moment as it passes, embrace all that life has to offer and to celebrate the joy of everyday. The hummingbird's delicate grace reminds us that life is rich, beauty is everywhere, every personal connection has meaning and that laughter is life's sweetest creation.*"

~ Papyrus

Be strong and courageous, be without fear, for the Lord your God will be with you, wherever you go.

~ Joshua 1:9

*About
the Author*

Jacqueline Dunkle

a licensed Massage Therapist & Bodyworker
with an Associates Business Degree
uses a unique combination of modalities as an
Intuitive Healing Coach to address
body, mind and spirit.
A former native of Pennsylvania,
she now resides in North Carolina.

  Paralyzed Without Fear

www.ParalyzedWithoutFear.com